Content

Why the Big Mo[1] approach?

Many 5 ☆☆☆☆☆ Reviews on Amazon and Google!

Testimonials: Strongly recommend **(Apple)** Very knowledgeable **(Oracle)** Explains our tech **(Google)** Excellent **(WSJ)** Gives 100% **(Sky)** Second to none **(News Inc.)** Good thinker **(BBC)** Highly interactive **(Springer)** Our specialist **(Hearst)** Delightful! **(ON24)** The best! **(TV NZ)** Entrepreneurial **(London Live TV)** Highly successful **(Virgin)** Fantastic! **(Mondelez Cadburys)** High acumen **(Lenovo)** Expert consultant **(SunnyD)** Innovator **(Kraft Heinz)** Influencer **(Mr Muscle JW)** Top bloke **(Kia/Hyundai)** Illuminating! **(Unipart)** Brilliant **(Eurotunnel)** De-mystifies! **(NHS)** Worth hearing **(Publicis)** Top trainer **(Havas)** Thought leader **(WPP)** Visionary **(Omnicom)** Expert speaker **(Direct Marketing Assoc)** Expert Fellow **(Institute of Direct & Digital Marketing)** Top expert **(PR & Comms Assoc)** Top speaker **(Hotel Booking Assoc)** Our expert Fellow **(Chartered Institute of Marketing)** Recognised Fellow **(Royal Soc for Arts & Commerce)** Enlightening! **(British Council)**

---

[1] https://www.linkedin.com/in/mauricebigmoflynn/

BE BETTER BUSINESS

A STEP BY STEP GUIDE

BY BIG MO FLYNN

WITH ILLUSTRATIONS BY DARA FLYNN

Maurice 'Big Mo' Flynn is recommended[2] by many of the tens of thousands of business executives, whom he has helped to improve their businesses, from companies including **Google, Oracle, Apple, the BBC, Sky, WPP, Omnicom, Havas, P&G, Nestle, Unilever, Coca Cola, Audi, Kia/Hyundai, Nissan, L'Oreal, Kraft Heinz, British Airways & many more.** Many years ago Maurice graduated top of his college in engineering & data at

---

[2] https://www.linkedin.com/in/mauricebigmoflynn/

Cambridge University. His family originally came to the UK in 1971 as refugees from the war in Northern Ireland.

Introduction to Be Better Business

"I have spent the **past 30 years advising thousands of companies and tens of thousands of business executives** - from CEO's of Fortune 500 companies to graduate recruits and "one man band" startups - **how to make their businesses better using low cost but intelligent, data led techniques**. Over the years I've repeatedly seen the new business techniques and approaches I've proposed to my clients, **move from early 'visionary thinking' stage to accepted mainstream and profitable business practice**. In the early stages of many such techniques, I'll openly admit my ideas have sometimes been **rejected by over comfortable, board level directors who 'knew better based on gut feel'.** I understand human nature and bear no grudges :) but it's nice to have been **proved right repeatedly over the years - as my many client testimonials bear witness to**. Not always of course! Having now completed many tens of thousands of hours of project delivery, training events, presentation/book writing and speech making on these topics, **I decided to start to distill my know how into this series of books,** of which this one comes first. In the process of summarising this book's content, I wanted to make it as simple as possible, yet without losing all the detail necessary to follow the advice given. Here therefore is a summary of many of the **ways I've helped businesses improve in the last few years**. It's relevant for everyone really - from **savvy tech startups to corporate behemoths and everything in between** - and I've worked for them all! It covers hot newer topics like **Data Privacy and GDPR** in great detail as I've focused a lot on that recently. It also covers more 'traditional' areas of improvement, where there's still a lot to be gained, like **Digital Business Transformation and Social Media (Facebook etc.)**. This book distils both my direct business and project experience as well as **insights curated from my own trusted, proven and expert sources**, all of whom are fully referenced in the text. It should therefore be helpful for all levels of experience from **beginner to expert**. I have tried to deliver a partly multimedia experience with links to **related videos online, which can be viewed in parallel**. Book owners are always welcome to contact me with follow up **questions via social media**. You can also request from me **editable, digital copies of the document templates shown in the book, on a complimentary basis**."

Disclaimer & dedications

<u>Disclaimer</u>: I'm not a lawyer so cannot dispense legal advice!

These are the **collective opinions of Maurice 'Big Mo' Flynn** based on 30 years of relevant working experience and a **lifetime of learning and working with like minded experts**. They are therefore **not meant to be 100% perfect for everyone** - they are **simply meant to be generally useful!** They are especially relevant for **companies with limited resources** who are looking for a common sense and **cost effective approach**.

Dedicated to my mother, sister and brothers who never stop moving forward. Plus my wife and sons who get me out of bed in the morning, whether I want to or not. :)

Be Better Business 1: Data Privacy & GDPR

Ready steady ... go!

We **can't be a better business if we're non compliant** and GDPR is one of the biggest compliance challenges of the year.

This information is curated from the **still evolving advice of the top experts** - e.g. the ICO[3] (Information Commissioner's Office) with **their "12 step framework[4]"** - allied with hands on GDPR preparation project experience with 50+ companies. Overall the aim is to deliver an approach that is "**as simple as possible**" and helps delivers "**project to do checklists**" which are widely applicable and as easy as possible to understand as per guidelines. Do feedback as to how well this approach meets your needs?

But first let's watch this ...

---

[3] "ICO: Home." https://ico.org.uk/. Accessed 10 Jun. 2018.
[4] https://ico.org.uk/media/1624219/preparing-for-the-gdpr-12-steps.pdf

9

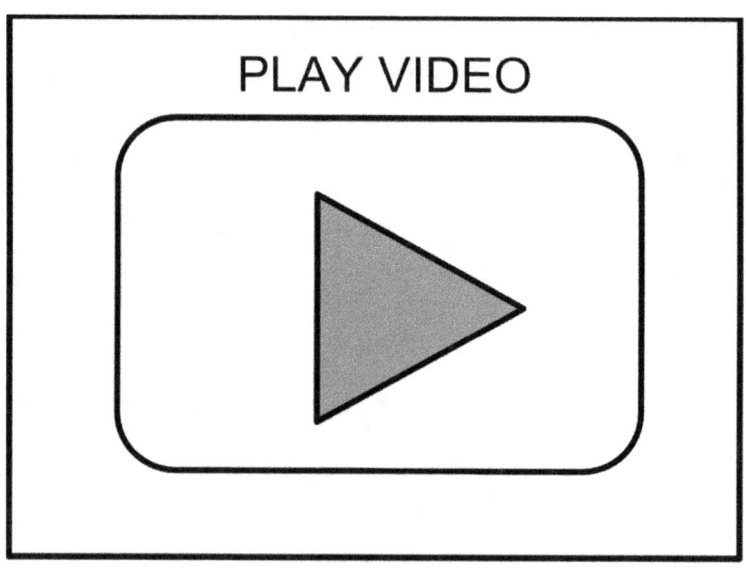

[VIDEO: https://www.youtube.com/watch?v=KzM-XLwgfAc]

So what have you heard about GDPR[5]? There is a lot of confusion, partly because some of the rules will **ultimately be clarified in the law courts**. But we can't wait around for that. We aim here to **focus on the essential business needs,** as closely as possible.

As you will see, we break the information into 4 sections throughout, starting with **general introductory information, followed by GDPR specifics and finally "what the experts say" summaries.** In the appendices you will also find the **key policies, processes and template documents, which help companies with**

---

[5] "Data protection | European Commission." 9 Jan. 2018,
https://ec.europa.eu/info/law/law-topic/data-protection_en. Accessed 10 Jun. 2018.

limited resources prepare for GDPR more quickly and efficiently. They are based on a common approach that is curated from the insights and experience of **multiple expert, trusted sources, allied with real life, GDPR preparation, project management experience**[6].

What the experts say:

Initial insights into better GDPR preparation:

1. Key principles for GDPR preparation are **1a. Data Privacy Management Involves Everyone**[7]: i.e. these activities are understood and embedded throughout the organisation; **1b. We Take Responsibility:** i.e. key activities are implemented and maintained by each business, acting for themselves; **1c. We Evidence:** i.e. this activity produces documentary evidence that we retain to demonstrate our accountability and compliance.

2. Companies have been worried by the threat of fines of up to €20 million or 4% of total worldwide annual turnover[8] of the preceding financial year, but the ICO has been clear that these '12 step' compliance efforts will

---

[6] " Maurice 'Big Mo' Flynn FCIM CMPRCA - GM - Breathe ... - LinkedIn."
https://uk.linkedin.com/in/mauricebigmoflynn. Accessed 10 Jun. 2018.
[7] "Preparing for the General Data Protection Regulation (GDPR) 12 ... - ICO."
https://ico.org.uk/media/1624219/preparing-for-the-gdpr-12-steps.pdf. Accessed 10 Jun. 2018.
[8] "The principles | ICO."
https://ico.org.uk/for-organisations/guide-to-the-general-data-protection-regulation-gdpr/principles/.
Accessed 10 Jun. 2018.

mitigate any penalties[9] (Ref: GDPR Article 83[10]). There is also the risk of **liability to 'data subjects'** if data leaks lead to financial or reputational damage. That situation would be resolved in a court of law and normally would depend on to what extent compliance efforts and damages could be proven (Ref: GDPR Article 82[11]).

3. Existing laws: We have plenty of laws that we currently follow and most of those continue of course. We just need to **adjust our approach to take GDPR into account e.g. Employment contracts** (Ref: GDPR Article 88[12]), National ID's (Ref: GDPR Article 87[13]), Freedom of expression (Ref: GDPR Article 85[14]).

4. There is **another body of law on the horizon which is often called "E-Privacy[15]"** which - once finalised - will **overlay and intersect with GDPR** rules in some areas **eg email, cookies, ads and more**. However it's still in consultation stage and experts **don't expect it to be**

---

[9] "Data Protection Reform: What to be aware of – CASE Europe – Medium." 11 Oct. 2016, https://medium.com/@CASE_Europe/data-protection-reform-what-to-be-aware-of-5e137e5dce15. Accessed 10 Jun. 2018.
[10] "Article 83 EU General Data Protection Regulation (EU-GDPR). Privacy ...." http://www.privacy-regulation.eu/en/article-83-general-conditions-for-imposing-administrative-fines-GDPR.htm. Accessed 10 Jun. 2018.
[11] "Article 82 EU General Data Protection Regulation (EU-GDPR). Privacy ...." http://www.privacy-regulation.eu/en/article-82-right-to-compensation-and-liability-GDPR.htm. Accessed 10 Jun. 2018.
[12] "Article 88 EU General Data Protection Regulation (EU-GDPR). Privacy ...." http://www.privacy-regulation.eu/en/article-88-processing-in-the-context-of-employment-GDPR.htm. Accessed 10 Jun. 2018.
[13] "Article 87 EU General Data Protection Regulation (EU-GDPR). Privacy ...." http://www.privacy-regulation.eu/en/article-87-processing-of-the-national-identification-number-GDPR.htm. Accessed 10 Jun. 2018.
[14] "Article 85 EU General Data Protection Regulation (EU-GDPR). Privacy ...." http://www.privacy-regulation.eu/en/article-85-processing-and-freedom-of-expression-and-information-GDPR.htm. Accessed 10 Jun. 2018.
[15] "ePrivacy Regulation (European Union) - Wikipedia." https://en.wikipedia.org/wiki/EPrivacy_Regulation_(European_Union). Accessed 10 Jun. 2018.

finalised before the summer this year, and could easily slip to a later date. So watch this space!

OK so far? Good - then let's get going next with the first of the "12 steps for GDPR preparation!"

1.1 Training & awareness

Raise what?

Better businesses need relevant and flexible training programmes. In this case we need to raise awareness of GDPR amongst our **senior management** as they are key to making change happen and allocating resources. We then need to raise awareness amongst our **employees and close partners, who come into contact with personal data**. Finally we need to raise **general awareness of the need for better personal data privacy practices for all our employees,** to minimise the risks of human error, as well as document our commitment and compliance.

So let's recap the basics ...

1. The General Data Protection Regulation (GDPR)[16] is a **regulation (i.e. legal)** by which the EU governing bodies will **strengthen and unify personal data protection**. It became applicable on **25/05/2018** and involves **all personal data of living people in the EU/EEA[17].** Some experts argue it also covers all personal data processed in that region but for now the main focus of the authorities is residents' data.

2. Therefore it's relevant to **all companies dealing with people's data from the EU/EEA,** directly or via partners. This includes **data controllers (who gather the data from real people) as well as data processors[18] (who use personal data under the terms and conditions from**

---

16 "General Data Protection Regulation - Wikipedia."
https://en.wikipedia.org/wiki/General_Data_Protection_Regulation. Accessed 11 Jun. 2018.
17 "European Economic Area - Wikipedia." https://en.wikipedia.org/wiki/European_Economic_Area. Accessed 11 Jun. 2018.
18 "All you need to know about GDPR Controllers and Processors - Medium." 12 Sep. 2017, https://medium.com/@sagaraq/all-you-need-to-know-about-gdpr-controllers-and-processors-248200ef4126. Accessed 11 Jun. 2018.

other companies). Also Data Protection Officers[19] are mandatory for bigger companies to ensure compliance. Pre and post Brexit[20] the UK government has confirmed alignment with GDPR.

Note: EU: Austria, Belgium, Bulgaria, Croatia, Republic of Cyprus, Czech Republic, Denmark, Estonia, Finland, France, Germany, Greece, Hungary, Ireland, Italy, Latvia, Lithuania, Luxembourg, Malta, Netherlands, Poland, Portugal, Romania, Slovakia, Slovenia, Spain, Sweden and the UK. EEA: Iceland, Liechtenstein and Norway.

What the experts say:

Across most industries, GDPR experts are recommending **intensive, specialist training for Data Protection Officers, tailored training events** for personal data handlers and general staff, plus **refreshers** ensuring ongoing improvement and compliance documentation. Internal tracking of **key compliance performance metrics as well as ongoing documentary evidencing** is essential. As an add on, **independent auditing and stress testing of compliance processes ensures a reduced risk approach.**

---

[19] "Art. 39 GDPR – Tasks of the data protection officer | General Data ...." https://gdpr-info.eu/art-39-gdpr/. Accessed 11 Jun. 2018.
[20] "Brexit GDPR What to Expect in 2018 | Shearman & Sterling." 3 Jan. 2018, https://www.shearman.com/perspectives/2018/01/brexit-and-gdpr-what-to-expect-in-2018. Accessed 11 Jun. 2018.

OK so all that **sounds fine in theory but how do we actually do this in practice**, with multiple colleagues and partners? Below you'll find the **templates I've created for the policies and procedures needed, as well as the reference and evidence documentation required**, to help make this process manageable.

Step 1: Guides & documentation

Policy	**At Company X Ltd. we acknowledge that training our employees about the importance of protecting the privacy of people's personal data is essential under GDPR and helps us improve our business performance in general.** We are committed to ensuring people's personal data is managed competently by us via: • Ensuring compliance with all relevant legislation as a minimum. • Setting and reviewing performance against objectives and targets that drive continuous improvements in our compliance in this area. • Providing sufficient information, resources and training to facilitate the achievement of our objectives in this area. Overall responsibility for data privacy and protection in line with GDPR rests with the board of directors. The board of directors discharges this responsibility through the departmental teams who are responsible for the implementation of this Policy. This Policy statement applies to the whole of Company X Ltd.and is available to all employees via our internal file system. Our privacy policy is also made publicly available on our website. The contents of this Policy will be reviewed and updated as necessary and on at least an annual basis.

Procedure	• By xx/xx/2018 - Led by Director & Consultant:
	    ○ Senior management training
	    ○ Personal data handler & GDPR policy/procedure training inc. handbook
	    ○ All staff education session
	    ○ Simple audit of privacy by design
	• June - Dec 2018 - Led by Director:
	    ○ Refresher internal comms on key GDPR compliance messages
	    ○ Occasional internal "spot & stress testing"
	    ○ Review emergent "best practice" monthly via ICO and optimise
	    ○ Incorporate into new employee onboarding, staff CPD and employee leaving processes
	• 2019 - Led by Director:
	    ○ Continue with above procedures
	    ○ Review & Incorporate e-Privacy law changes into GDPR compliance policy and procedures

References & Resources	PRIMARY: ICO: • https://ico.org.uk/for-organisations/guide-to-the-general-data-protection-regulation-gdpr/ • https://ico.org.uk/media/1624219/preparing-for-the-gdpr-12-steps.pdf CIPD:

- https://www.cipd.co.uk/knowledge/fundamentals/people/hr/policies-factsheet

SECONDARY:

External Consultant:

- https://www.linkedin.com/in/mauricebigmoflynn

Books:

- https://www.amazon.co.uk/-/e/B078ZGGLCW

Video:

- https://www.youtube.com/watch?v=KzM-XLwgfAc

Document Control Reference: GDPR - Issue No: v1.1 - Issue Date: xx/xx/2018 -Review Date: xx/xx/2019

Signature 1: *NAME 1* - Data Privacy & Protection Lead

Signature 2: *NAME 2* - Director

Company X Ltd., ADDRESS, UK +44 (0)TELEPHONE NUMBER.

Step 1: Guides & documentation

Subject	Last Completed	Next Date Planned
DPO Training	NA [Note: We are under 250 staff and use very small amounts of non sensitive, personal data]	NA [Note: We are under 250 staff and use very small amounts of non sensitive, personal data]
Senior Management	Date:xx/xx/2018	Monthly internal reminder emails planned
Personal Data Handlers	Date:xx/xx/2018	Monthly internal reminder emails planned
All Staff and Partners	Date:xx/xx/2018	Monthly internal reminder emails planned
Board GDPR Performance Review	The GDPR prep project is managed by the Data Privacy and Protection Lead and the CEO supported by a consultant.	The GDPR prep project is managed by the Data Privacy and Protection Lead and the CEO supported by a consultant.
GDPR Compliance Audit **& Procedure Practice**	Date: xx/xx/2018	Review planned forxx/xx/2018

Document Control Reference: GDPR - Issue No: v1.1 - Issue Date: xx/xx/2018 -Review Date: xx/xx/2019

Signature 1: *Name 1* - Data Privacy & Protection Lead

Signature 2: *Name 2* - Director

Company X Ltd., ADDRESS, UK +44 (0)TELEPHONE NUMBER.

CPD certificate of completion

I'm delighted to certify that the persons named below, on the following date and location:

Name List - Location - Date

Attended and successfully completed my training event(s)

"Preparing for GDPR & Optimising Digital Channels in a Post GDPR World" run by Maurice 'Big Mo' Flynn

The content for my training events is based on the guidelines from the Information Commissioner's Office plus other expert sources. It is also reviewed, approved and accredited by a professional UK teacher.

Signed:

Maurice 'Big Mo' Flynn

GDPR Prep Trainer & Author   Professional UK Teacher

And that's step 1 done! Feeling more confident? Well then let's crack on with the next step below.

1.2 Project & team resourcing

Who's in charge?

Without resources nothing will happen so we can't get to be better businesses! This section therefore is about how we structure and resource our GDPR team and project. Bigger companies (250+ employees) using lots of personal data are **compelled to have a data protection officer**[21]. Smaller companies are not compelled but some of the principles of the role help **avoid the risks** associated with GDPR compliance **e.g. clear ownership of the challenges plus clear lines of communication**. Companies need to assess the mandatories and risks involved and **look at their in house vs outsourced requirements.**

Tell me officer?

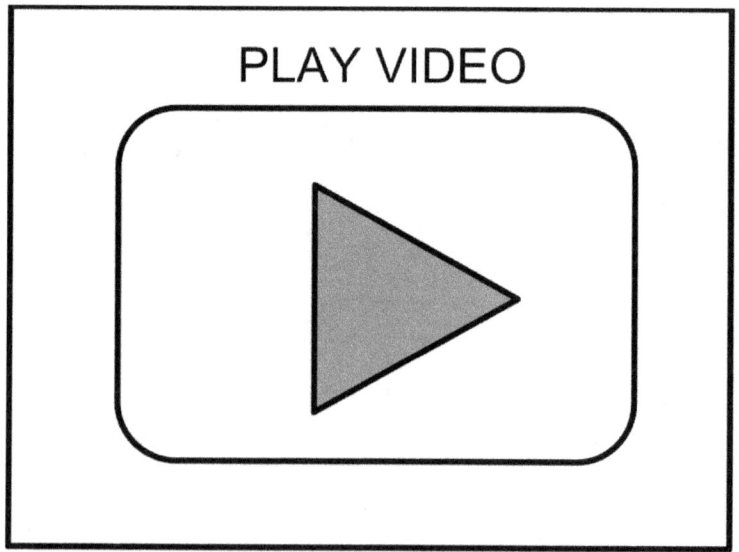

[VIDEO: https://www.youtube.com/watch?v=-fLITVXBxYo]

---

[21] "What is a Data Protection Officer (DPO)? Learn About the New Role ...." 30 Jan. 2017, https://digitalguardian.com/blog/what-data-protection-officer-dpo-learn-about-new-role-required-gdpr-compliance. Accessed 10 Jun. 2018.

A DPO is mandatory for **public bodies, large users of sensitive data and those undertaking large scale, regular and systematic monitoring of data subjects**[22]. Many larger companies also find it the best way to manage the GDPR risks, requirements and new processes, **ensuring ownership**. The DPO should be a data privacy law **expert**[23], advising all involved parties re their **data protection obligations**, monitoring **compliance, assigning project responsibilities** plus supporting training and auditing activities. The DPO should also advise on and lead **DPIA impact assessments**[24], cooperating with and contacting the **supervisory authority**[25] **and data subjects**[26] as required, be involved in **all issues** relating to processing personal data, ensure **sufficient resources** while acting in an **independent** manner, with clear reporting to the **highest management level.** It is therefore not a role to be allocated lightly to a newest member of staff.

---

[22] "Data Protection Officer – do you need to appoint one? - PwC UK blogs." 17 Feb. 2017, http://pwc.blogs.com/data_protection/2017/02/data-protection-officer-do-you-need-to-appoint-one.html. Accessed 10 Jun. 2018.
[23] "Data protection officers | ICO." https://ico.org.uk/for-organisations/guide-to-the-general-data-protection-regulation-gdpr/accountability-and-governance/data-protection-officers/. Accessed 10 Jun. 2018.
[24] "Sample DPIA template - ICO." 8 Mar. 2018, https://ico.org.uk/media/about-the-ico/consultations/2258461/dpia-template-v04-post-comms-review-20180308.pdf. Accessed 10 Jun. 2018.
[25] "Art. 51 GDPR – Supervisory authority | General Data Protection ...." https://gdpr-info.eu/art-51-gdpr/. Accessed 10 Jun. 2018.
[26] "What is a data subject? - EU GDPR Compliant." https://eugdprcompliant.com/what-is-data-subject/. Accessed 10 Jun. 2018.

What the experts say:

For larger companies, having a DPO **ensures ownership** of the responsibilities of GDPR compliance. The role should be **in house if resources allow, but can be contracted out if resources/expertise are lacking.**

For smaller companies there may not be enough work for a full time DPO. **In this case a well resourced cross functional team, with a clearly identified team leader plus senior management sponsorship, should suffice**[27].

This is addressed in GDPR Articles 38[28] and 39[29].

OK so all that **sounds fine in theory but how do we actually do this in practice**, with multiple colleagues and partners? Below you'll find the **templates I've created for the policies and procedures needed, as well as the reference and evidence documentation required**, to help make this process manageable.

---

27 "How to create a cross-functional GDPR implementation team: PwC."
https://www.pwc.com/us/en/increasing-it-effectiveness/publications/create-cross-functional-gdpr-implementation-team.html. Accessed 10 Jun. 2018.
28 "Art. 38 GDPR – Position of the data protection officer | General Data ...."
https://gdpr-info.eu/art-38-gdpr/. Accessed 10 Jun. 2018.
29 "Art. 39 GDPR – Tasks of the data protection officer | General Data ...."
https://gdpr-info.eu/art-39-gdpr/. Accessed 10 Jun. 2018.

Policy	**At Company X Ltd. we acknowledge that ensuring a clear understanding of how GDPR projects are best resourced and project teams structured - including whether an in house DPO is mandatory or helpful - is essential under GDPR and helps us improve our business performance in general.** We are committed to ensuring people's personal data is managed competently by us via: <ul><li>Ensuring compliance with all relevant legislation as a minimum.</li><li>Setting and reviewing performance against objectives and targets that drive continuous improvements in our compliance in this area.</li><li>Providing sufficient information, resources and training to facilitate the achievement of our objectives in this area.</li></ul>Overall responsibility for data privacy and protection in line with GDPR rests with the board of directors. The board of directors discharges this responsibility through the departmental teams who are responsible for the implementation of this Policy. This Policy statement applies to the whole of Company X Ltd.and is available to all employees via our internal file system. Our privacy policy is also made publicly available on our website. The contents of this Policy will be reviewed and updated as necessary and on at least an annual basis.
Procedure	<ul><li>Annual cycle:<ul><li>Our company will review the resourcing for the GDPR prep and maintenance projects and revise as appropriate.</li><li>Data Protection Officer: N/A as we are under 250 staff & process small amounts of personal data.</li><li>Data Privacy & Protection Lead:<ul><li>Name: NAME 1</li><li>Role: Communicate re GDPR issues throughout the company and escalate issues for resolution.</li><li>Resource: 5% of time</li><li>Support: by staff/contractors in charge of HR, IT, Marketing, Sales, Finance, Legal, Other.</li></ul></li><li>Data controllers collect the personal data and/or set the terms of the related privacy policy. Data processors use data from controllers and follow their T&Cs. **Data controllers need to register with the ICO unless they are exempt - see https://ico.org.uk/for-organisations/register/self-assessment**</li></ul></li><li>Quarterly cycle:<ul><li>Our Data Privacy & Protection Lead will review the resourcing for the GDPR prep and maintenance projects and recommend revisions as appropriate to the directors.</li></ul></li></ul>

References & Resources	**PRIMARY:** **ICO:** • https://ico.org.uk/for-organisations/guide-to-the-general-data-protection-regulation-gdpr/accountability-and-governance/data-protection-officers • https://ico.org.uk/for-organisations/guide-to-the-general-data-protection-regulation-gdpr/ • https://ico.org.uk/media/1624219/preparing-for-the-gdpr-12-steps.pdf **CIPD:** • https://www.cipd.co.uk/knowledge/fundamentals/people/hr/policies-factsheet

Document Control Reference: GDPR - Issue No: v1.1 - Issue Date: xx/xx/2018 -Review Date: xx/xx/2019

Signature 1: *Name 1* - Data Privacy & Protection Lead

Signature 2: *Name 2* - Director

Company X Ltd., ADDRESS, UK +44 (0)TELEPHONE NUMBER.

Still feeling confident? Well let's crack on with the next step!

1.3 Data and risk audit

You are being audited

Simply put, this means we need to **document all the personal data**[30] we have and use, anywhere in our

[30] "4 steps to conducting a GDPR compliance audit | Information ...." 14 Aug. 2017,
https://www.information-management.com/opinion/4-steps-to-conducting-a-gdpr-compliance-audit.
Accessed 10 Jun. 2018.

business or partner businesses. This personal data will be stored in a variety of places, including **official data storage facilities and informal places** e.g. on personal computers and mobile devices. It also means **non digital data** e.g. old reports and other documents. Just to reiterate we also need to include personal data that comes from or is shared **with business partners**. We need to **assess the GDPR compliance risks involved and then plan to minimise**[31].

What's personal?

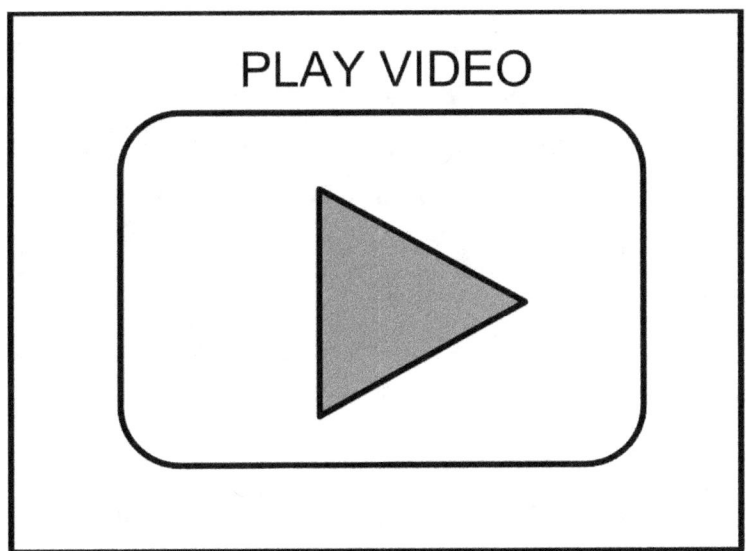

[VIDEO from Timecode 00:53: https://vimeo.com/230965114]

---

[31] "The Risk-Based Approach in the GDPR: Interpretation and Implications."
https://iapp.org/resources/article/the-risk-based-approach-in-the-gdpr-interpretation-and-implications/.
Accessed 10 Jun. 2018.

Personal data is any data that can be used to **identify an individual person**[32]. However it **doesn't just mean obvious stuff** like email addresses and mobile phone numbers. It also includes **any** data that could be used to identify someone even indirectly **eg IP address and pseudonyms.** For all personal data we need to record **what permissions/privacy notices were given** for that data and **if/when they expire.** We also need to answer some questions related to **how the data can be found, shared, amended and deleted**[33].

What the experts say:

There is an **ongoing debate amongst experts** as to how to interpret these new rules for different businesses, as well as the exact meaning of the terms used. As always it's **probably safest to "assume the worst"**[34] and plan for that but an intelligent and informed approach is still needed, **to avoid commercially undermining our business models.**

The audit and risk document coming out of this step **should be a topline summary,** otherwise it will be too hard to **understand, use and update**. This reflected in

---

[32] "Art. 4 GDPR – Definitions | General Data Protection Regulation (GDPR)." https://gdpr-info.eu/art-4-gdpr/. Accessed 10 Jun. 2018.

[33] "GDPR: Carrying Out your First Data Audit - Mewburn Ellis." 29 Jan. 2018, http://mewburn.com/gdpr-carrying-out-your-first-data-audit/. Accessed 10 Jun. 2018.

[34] "The Nightmare Letter: A Subject Access Request Under GDPR ...." 17 Mar. 2018, https://news.ycombinator.com/item?id=16606629. Accessed 10 Jun. 2018.

examples we can see from the public sector e.g. Gov.uk/government/publications/IAR.[35]

OK so all that **sounds fine in theory but how do we actually do this in practice**, with multiple colleagues and partners? Below you'll find the **templates I've created for the policies and procedures needed, as well as the reference and evidence documentation required**, to help make this process manageable.

---

[35] "Advice 39 Developing an Information Asset Register." https://www.informationstrategy.tas.gov.au/Records-Management-Principles/Document%20Library%20%20Tools/Advice%2039%20Developing%20an%20Information%20Asset%20Register.pdf. Accessed 10 Jun. 2018.

Policy	**At Company X Ltd. we acknowledge that auditing the personal data we use and assessing then tackling the risks of non compliance is essential under GDPR and helps us improve our business performance in general.** We are committed to ensuring people's personal data is managed competently by us via: • Ensuring compliance with all relevant legislation as a minimum. • Setting and reviewing performance against objectives and targets that drive continuous improvements in our compliance in this area. • Providing sufficient information, resources and training to facilitate the achievement of our objectives in this area. Overall responsibility for data privacy and protection in line with GDPR rests with the board of directors. The board of directors discharges this responsibility through the departmental teams who are responsible for the implementation of this Policy. This Policy statement applies to the whole of Company X Ltd.and is available to all employees via our internal file system. Our privacy policy is also made publicly available on our website. The contents of this Policy will be reviewed and updated as necessary and on at least an annual basis.

Procedure	• Annual cycle:
	   ○ Our GDPR data privacy & protection lead with management will review and update the latest personal data audit and risk analysis on an annual basis.
	• Quarterly cycle:
	   ○ Our GDPR data privacy & protection lead with management will review the latest personal data audit and recommend if any elements need to be updated in advance of the next annual review.

References & Resources	**PRIMARY:** **ICO:** • https://ico.org.uk/for-organisations/guide-to-the-general-data-protection-regulation-gdpr/ • https://ico.org.uk/media/1624219/preparing-for-the-gdpr-12-steps.pdf **CIPD:** • https://www.cipd.co.uk/knowledge/fundamentals/people/hr/policies-factsheet **SECONDARY:** **Video:** • https://vimeo.com/230965114

34

External Consultant:

- https://www.linkedin.com/in/mauricebigmoflynn

Book:

- https://www.amazon.co.uk/-/e/B078ZGGLCW

Document Control Reference: GDPR - Issue No: v1.1 - Issue Date: xx/xx/2018 -Review Date: xx/xx/2019

Signature 1: *NAME 1* - Data Privacy & Protection Lead

Signature 2: *NAME 2* - Director

Company X Ltd., ADDRESS, UK +44 (0)TELEPHONE NUMBER.

Question?	Answer?	Contracted eg Customers Suppliers Partners	No Contract eg Sales & Marketing Prospects Recruitment Prospects	Contracted Employees
What?	1.Contact Information such as name, email, address, phone number and related data	YES/NO NOTES:	YES/NO NOTES:	YES/NO NOTES:
What?	2.Demographic information such as age, education, gender, interests and post code	YES/NO NOTES:	YES/NO NOTES:	YES/NO NOTES:
What?	3.Billing Information, such as bank account info, credit card number and billing address	YES/NO NOTES:	YES/NO NOTES:	YES/NO NOTES:
What?	4.Unique Identifiers, such as username, account number or password	YES/NO NOTES:	YES/NO NOTES:	YES/NO NOTES:
What?	5.Information about their business, such as company name, company size and business type	YES/NO NOTES:	YES/NO NOTES:	YES/NO NOTES:
What?	6.Click data such as Internet protocol (IP) address, browser type, Internet service provider (ISP), referring/exit pages, the files viewed on our site (e.g., HTML pages, graphics, etc.), operating system, device identifiers, date/time stamp, clickstreams, cookies or similar technologies	YES/NO NOTES:	YES/NO NOTES:	YES/NO NOTES:
What?	7.Images & video content inc. CCTV	YES/NO NOTES:	YES/NO NOTES:	YES/NO NOTES:
What?	8.Special category & sensitive data ie children; race; ethnic origin; politics; religion; trade union membership; genetics; biometrics (where used for ID purposes); health; sex life; or sexual orientation; criminal records.	YES/NO NOTES:	YES/NO NOTES:	YES/NO NOTES:
From?	1.Data subject	YES/NO NOTES:	YES/NO NOTES:	YES/NO NOTES:
From?	2.Partner business	YES/NO NOTES:	YES/NO NOTES:	YES/NO NOTES:
From?	3.Other eg government, local authority,	YES/NO	YES/NO	YES/NO

	family member	NOTES:	NOTES:	NOTES:
Use =Retention time (Country)	1.Contract & service comms	YES/NO = Retention time (Country)	YES/NO = Retention time (Country)	YES/NO = Retention time (Country)
Use =Duration (Country)	2.Research & service improvement	YES/NO = Retention time (Country)	YES/NO = Retention time (Country)	YES/NO = Retention time (Country)
Use +Duration (Country)	3.Identification & authentication	YES/NO = Retention time (Country)	YES/NO = Retention time (Country)	YES/NO = Retention time (Country)
Use +Duration (Country)	4.Billing, payment & financial reporting	YES/NO = Retention time (Country)	YES/NO = Retention time (Country)	YES/NO = Retention time (Country)
Use +Duration (Country)	5.Marketing & related comms	YES/NO = Retention time (Country)	YES/NO = Retention time (Country)	YES/NO = Retention time (Country)
Use +Duration (Country)	6.Sensitive data checks	YES/NO = Retention time (Country)	YES/NO = Retention time (Country)	YES/NO = Retention time (Country)
Use +Duration (Country)	7.Automated profiling & decision making	YES/NO = Retention time (Country)	YES/NO = Retention time (Country)	YES/NO = Retention time (Country)
Legal?	1.Contract	YES/NO NOTES:	YES/NO NOTES:	YES/NO NOTES:
Legal?	2.Legal obligation inc. for special category (i.e sensitive) data	YES/NO NOTES:	YES/NO NOTES:	YES/NO NOTES:
Legal?	3.Legitimate interest	YES/NO NOTES:	YES/NO NOTES:	YES/NO NOTES:
Legal?	4.Consent (inc. for childrens' data)	YES/NO NOTES:	YES/NO NOTES:	YES/NO NOTES:
Legal?	5.Public task eg public sector, law courts, scientific research	YES/NO NOTES:	YES/NO NOTES:	YES/NO NOTES:
Legal?	6.Vital interests eg medical emergency	YES/NO NOTES:	YES/NO NOTES:	YES/NO NOTES:
Legal?	7. Special category (i.e sensitive) data	YES/NO NOTES:	YES/NO NOTES:	YES/NO NOTES:

Access?	1.Finance	YES/NO NOTES:	YES/NO NOTES:	YES/NO NOTES:
Access?	2.HR	YES/NO NOTES:	YES/NO NOTES:	YES/NO NOTES:
Access?	3.IT	YES/NO NOTES:	YES/NO NOTES:	YES/NO NOTES:
Access?	4.Sales & customer service	YES/NO NOTES:	YES/NO NOTES:	YES/NO NOTES:
Access?	5.Marketing & product/service development	YES/NO NOTES:	YES/NO NOTES:	YES/NO NOTES:
Shared?	1.Partner business	YES/NO NOTES:	YES/NO NOTES:	YES/NO NOTES:
Shared?	2.Other eg government, local authority	YES/NO NOTES:	YES/NO NOTES:	YES/NO NOTES:
Where?	1.In office central system/server/databases (Country?)	YES/NO NOTES:	YES/NO NOTES:	YES/NO NOTES:
Where?	2.In office devices eg desktops (Country?)	YES/NO NOTES:	YES/NO NOTES:	YES/NO NOTES:
Where?	3.In office paper archives (Country?)	YES/NO NOTES:	YES/NO NOTES:	YES/NO NOTES:
Where?	4.On portable devices eg laptops, mobiles	YES/NO NOTES:	YES/NO NOTES:	YES/NO NOTES:
Where?	5.3rd party paper archives (Country?)	YES/NO NOTES:	YES/NO NOTES:	YES/NO NOTES:
Where?	6.Cloud systems/data centres (Country?)	YES/NO NOTES:	YES/NO NOTES:	YES/NO NOTES:
Protect?	1.Secure premises (physical locks & alarms where necessary)	YES/NO NOTES:	YES/NO NOTES:	YES/NO NOTES:
Protect?	2.Best practice IT protection (eg Firewall, hacker and data leakage alerts where necessary)	YES/NO NOTES:	YES/NO NOTES:	YES/NO NOTES:
Protect?	3.Strong passwords and "need to know" access	YES/NO NOTES:	YES/NO NOTES:	YES/NO NOTES:
Protect?	3.Pseudonymisation eg client & employee ID numbers on IT systems	YES/NO NOTES:	YES/NO NOTES:	YES/NO NOTES:
Protect?	4.Anonymisation ie group data so individual profiles hidden	YES/NO NOTES:	YES/NO NOTES:	YES/NO NOTES:

Protect?	5.Encryption ie when big data sets moved between secure locations	YES/NO NOTES:	YES/NO NOTES:	YES/NO NOTES:
Protect?	6.Secure deletion	YES/NO NOTES:	YES/NO NOTES:	YES/NO NOTES:
Protect?	7.Corporate policies	YES/NO NOTES:	YES/NO NOTES:	YES/NO NOTES:
Protect?	8.Partner contracts	YES/NO NOTES:	YES/NO NOTES:	YES/NO NOTES:
High Risk & Impact	1.IT hack	YES/NO NOTES:	YES/NO NOTES:	YES/NO NOTES:
High Risk & Impact	2.Physical break in	YES/NO NOTES:	YES/NO NOTES:	YES/NO NOTES:
High Risk & Impact	3.Malicious employee/visitor action	YES/NO NOTES:	YES/NO NOTES:	YES/NO NOTES:
High Risk & Impact	4.Human error eg lost device, email error etc	YES/NO NOTES:	YES/NO NOTES:	YES/NO NOTES:
Solutions	- Action 1 - Action 2 - Action 3 - Action 4 - Action 5	Date Date Date Date Date	Date Date Date Date Date	Date Date Date Date Date

Document Control Reference: GDPR - Issue No: v1.1 - Issue Date: xx/xx/2018 -Review Date: xx/xx/2019

Signature 1: *NAME 1* - Data Privacy & Protection Lead

Signature 2: *NAME 2* - Director

Company X Ltd., ADDRESS, UK +44 (0)TELEPHONE NUMBER.

Still feeling confident?

Well let's crack on with the next step!

1.4 Plan lawful basis for data

How do we do?

Companies holding and using personal data need to be be **clear on the lawful basis**[36] for doing so and **document** that for evidencing on request. Companies

---

[36] "Lawful basis for processing | ICO."
https://ico.org.uk/for-organisations/guide-to-the-general-data-protection-regulation-gdpr/lawful-basis-for-processing/. Accessed 10 Jun. 2018.

can **no longer keep records of personal data indefinitely** [37] or without detailed documentation as to why. **Individuals, supervisory bodies**[38] **(e.g. the ICO) and courts** all can request access to that information at short notice. We need to first understand **what is permitted** under GDPR and put in place the **people, processes and tools** to ensure compliance. All **employees and data sharing partners will need to understand** the new rules and processes in order to avoid risk of human error.

It's the law dude …

Companies are permitted to hold and use personal data under any one of the following bases[39]: if **Consent** is given from the individual concerned; under a **Contract** i.e. by legal agreement; under existing **Laws** e.g. employment law; if **Vital** eg for life-or-death scenarios; if needed for **Public Tasks or Interests** eg court cases or scientific research; if we can justify **Legitimate Interests** i.e. where we must **balance the legitimate interests and rights of all parties** e.g. the individual's **right to privacy** and businesses' **commercial need to communicate their solutions to business challenges** in a relevant way.

---

[37] "Privacy by design - Wikipedia." https://en.wikipedia.org/wiki/Privacy_by_design. Accessed 10 Jun. 2018.
[38] "Art. 51 GDPR – Supervisory authority | General Data Protection …." https://gdpr-info.eu/art-51-gdpr/. Accessed 10 Jun. 2018.
[39] "Art. 6 GDPR – Lawfulness of processing | General Data Protection …." https://gdpr-info.eu/art-6-gdpr/. Accessed 10 Jun. 2018.

What the experts say:

Many companies have captured personal data over many years but with little or poor quality **documentation of the legal bases e.g. consent.** Many companies have either centralised or scattered databases but in both cases there's usually lots of **different data from multiple sources intermingled**. This all need to be untangled and **cleaned up fast**!

This is addressed in GDPR Articles 5[40], 6[41].

OK so all that **sounds fine in theory but how do we actually do this in practice**, with multiple colleagues and partners? Below you'll find the **templates I've created for the policies and procedures needed, as well as the reference and evidence documentation required**, to help make this process manageable. These are also relevant for the next step.

---

[40] "Article 5 EU General Data Protection Regulation (EU-GDPR). Privacy ...."
http://www.privacy-regulation.eu/en/article-5-principles-relating-to-processing-of-personal-data-GDPR.htm. Accessed 10 Jun. 2018.
[41] "Article 6 EU General Data Protection Regulation (EU-GDPR). Privacy ...."
http://www.privacy-regulation.eu/en/article-6-lawfulness-of-processing-GDPR.htm. Accessed 10 Jun. 2018.

Policy	At Company X Ltd. we acknowledge that keeping personal data lawful basis and retention records is essential under GDPR and helps us improve our business performance in general. We are committed to ensuring people's personal data is managed competently by us via: • Ensuring compliance with all relevant legislation as a minimum. • Setting and reviewing performance against objectives and targets that drive continuous improvements in our compliance in this area. • Providing sufficient information, resources and training to facilitate the achievement of our objectives in this area. Overall responsibility for data privacy and protection in line with GDPR rests with the board of directors. The board of directors discharges this responsibility through the departmental teams who are responsible for the implementation of this Policy. This Policy statement applies to the whole of Company X Ltd.and is available to all employees via our internal file system. Our privacy policy is also made publicly available on our website. The contents of this Policy will be reviewed and updated as necessary and on at least an annual basis.

Procedure	• Annual cycle:
	  ○ Our Data Privacy & Protection Lead with management will review and update the latest personal data lawful basis and retention record.
	• Quarterly cycle:
	  ○ Our Data Privacy & Protection Lead with management will review the latest personal data lawful basis record and recommend if any elements need to be actioned in advance of the next annual review.

References & Resources	PRIMARY: ICO: • https://ico.org.uk/for-organisations/guide-to-the-general-data-protection-regulation-gdpr/ • https://ico.org.uk/media/1624219/preparing-for-the-gdpr-12-steps.pdf CIPD: • https://www.cipd.co.uk/knowledge/fundamentals/people/hr/policies-factsheet SECONDARY: External Consultant: • https://www.linkedin.com/in/mauricebigmoflynn

	Book:
	• https://www.amazon.co.uk/-/e/B078ZGGLCW

Document Control Reference: GDPR - Issue No: v1.1 - Issue Date: xx/xx/2018 -Review Date: xx/xx/2019

Signature 1: *NAME 1* - Data Privacy & Protection Lead

Signature 2: *NAME 2* - Director

Company X Ltd., ADDRESS, UK +44 (0)TELEPHONE NUMBER.

Steps 4 & 5: Guides & documentation

	Consent? + Evidence?	Contract? + Evidence?	Legitimate Interest? + Evidence?	Secure Deletion? + Evidence?
With Contract:				
- Customer	YES/NO +Evidence?	YES/NO +Evidence?	YES/NO +Evidence?	YES/NO +Evidence?
- Supplier	YES/NO +Evidence?	YES/NO +Evidence?	YES/NO +Evidence?	YES/NO +Evidence?
- Other Partner	YES/NO +Evidence?	YES/NO +Evidence?	YES/NO +Evidence?	YES/NO +Evidence?
- Employee	YES/NO +Evidence?	YES/NO +Evidence?	YES/NO +Evidence?	YES/NO +Evidence?
- Sales/Marketing Leads:				
-- As Processor	YES/NO +Evidence?	YES/NO +Evidence?	YES/NO +Evidence?	YES/NO +Evidence?
- Recruitment: -- As Processor	YES/NO +Evidence?	YES/NO +Evidence?	YES/NO +Evidence?	YES/NO +Evidence?I
No Contract: - Sales/ Marketing Leads:				
-- As controller	YES/NO +Evidence?	YES/NO +Evidence?	YES/NO +Evidence?	YES/NO +Evidence?
- Recruitment Leads: -- As controller	YES/NO +Evidence?	YES/NO +Evidence?	YES/NO +Evidence?	YES/NO +Evidence?

Document Control Reference: GDPR - Issue No: v1.1 - Issue Date: xx/xx/2018 -Review Date: xx/xx/2019

Signature 1: *NAME 1* - Data Privacy & Protection Lead

Signature 2: *NAME 1* - Director

Company X Ltd., ADDRESS, UK +44 (0)TELEPHONE NUMBER.

OK we're motoring now! So let's crack on with the next step.

1.5 Correct consent & legitimate interest

Yes please!

Many businesses use personal data which has been captured over months or years and has **poor quality consent documentation and/or unclear legitimate**

interest justification. Businesses can have centralised or scattered databases but all too often different **sources of data intermingle without restriction or controls**. All personal data that has not been correctly gathered under GDPR rules must be re-assessed. To do this we need to understand **what consent**[42] **and legitimate interest**[43] **means under GDPR and audit our data accordingly.** Compliant data can be used for **an agreed, reasonable but minimised time period. Non compliant data must be deleted or re-addressed.**

Was that a yes?

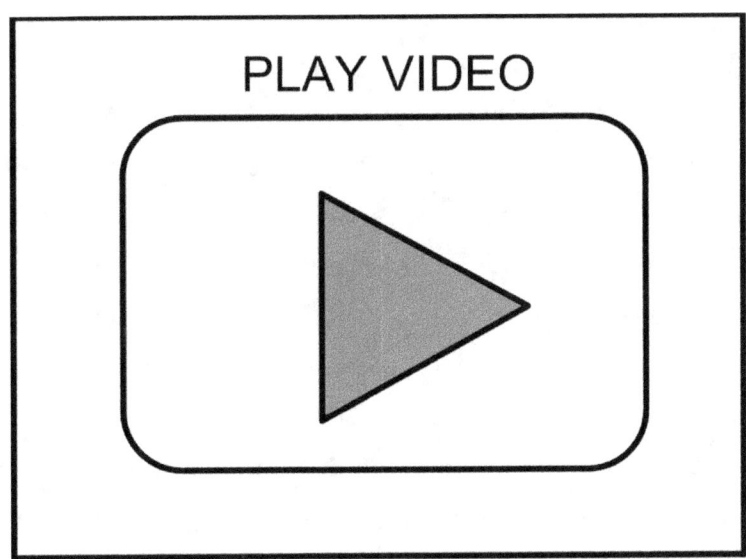

---

[42] "Art. 7 GDPR – Conditions for consent | General Data Protection ...." https://gdpr-info.eu/art-7-gdpr/. Accessed 10 Jun. 2018.
[43] "Legitimate interests | ICO."
https://ico.org.uk/for-organisations/guide-to-the-general-data-protection-regulation-gdpr/lawful-basis-for-processing/legitimate-interests/. Accessed 10 Jun. 2018.

[VIDEO: https://vimeo.com/196298299]

Under GDPR, consent[44] must be **freely given, specific, informed and unambiguous.** It requires a positive opt-in i.e. it **cannot be inferred** via pre ticked boxes and must be definitive. Consent agreements must be **separate from other T&C's** i.e. not hidden. It also must be **simple to withdraw** consent at any time. Legitimate interest[45] means we must **balance the legitimate interests and rights of all parties** e.g. the individual's **right to privacy** and businesses' **commercial interest in communicating their solutions in a relevant way**.

What the experts say:

As we all probably recognise many companies have personal data captured over the years with little or poor quality **documented consent nor legitimate use justification.** Many companies have generalised databases where lots of different **sources of data intermingle**. This all need to be untangled and **cleaned up fast!** Databases need to be segmented clearly into **sections, which are labelled with the different legal bases** by which we intend to use the personal data under GDPR. These segments need to be segmented

---

[44] "Explicit consent and how to obtain it - new GDPR consent guidelines." https://www.i-scoop.eu/gdpr/explicit-consent/. Accessed 10 Jun. 2018.
[45] "Legitimate Interest – GDPR EU.org." https://www.gdpreu.org/the-regulation/key-concepts/legitimate-interest/. Accessed 10 Jun. 2018.

again into **sub-sections i.e. compliant vs non compliant yet fixable vs non compliant not fixable therefore need to delete**.

This is addressed in Ref. GDPR Articles 5[46], 6[47] and 12[48].

OK so all that **sounds fine in theory but how do we actually do this in practice**, with multiple colleagues and partners? In the last as well as the next section you find the **templates I've created for the policies and procedures needed, as well as the reference and evidence documentation required**, to help make this process manageable.

[46] "Article 5 EU General Data Protection Regulation (EU-GDPR). Privacy ...."
http://www.privacy-regulation.eu/en/article-5-principles-relating-to-processing-of-personal-data-GDPR.htm. Accessed 10 Jun. 2018.
[47] "Article 6 EU General Data Protection Regulation (EU-GDPR). Privacy ...."
http://www.privacy-regulation.eu/en/article-6-lawfulness-of-processing-GDPR.htm. Accessed 10 Jun. 2018.
[48] "Article 12 EU General Data Protection Regulation (EU-GDPR). Privacy ...."
http://www.privacy-regulation.eu/en/article-12-transparent-information-communication-and-modalities-for-the-exercise-of-the-rights-of-the-data-subject-GDPR.htm. Accessed 10 Jun. 2018.

1.6 Privacy policies

That's private!

Under GDPR we have new rules regarding **privacy notices, policies and processes**[49] that we all need to take into account. Businesses **need to first understand**

---

[49] "Privacy policy - Wikipedia." https://en.wikipedia.org/wiki/Privacy_policy. Accessed 10 Jun. 2018.

these new requirements. Existing privacy notices require **amendments (e.g. on your website) and/or new ones written in their absence and for all places where personal data is taken.** All **employees and data sharing partners will to understand** the new rights and rules, to avoid risk of human error.

The changes ...

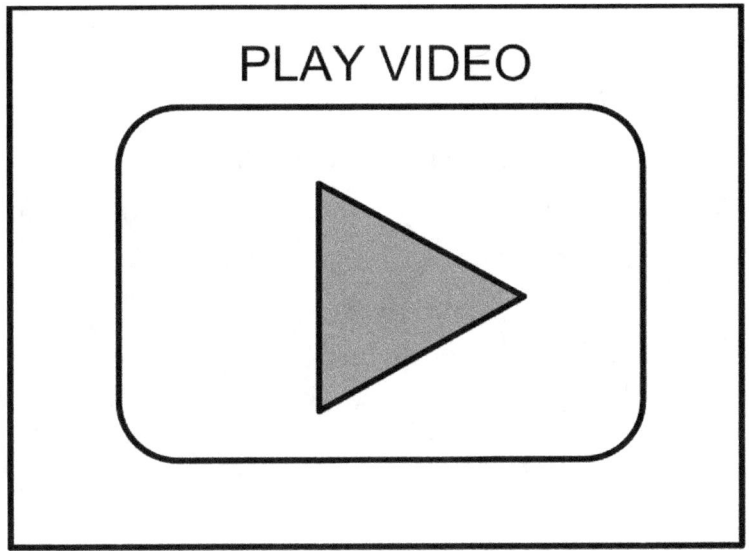

[VIDEO: https://www.youtube.com/watch?v=xIW5RI8K3Yg]

Privacy policies and notices need to communicate the **lawful basis/bases**[50] for collecting and processing personal data, as well as the proposed **retention**

---

[50] "Chapter 7: Lawful basis for processing – Unlocking the EU General ...." 13 Sep. 2017, https://www.whitecase.com/publications/article/chapter-7-lawful-basis-processing-unlocking-eu-gener al-data-protection. Accessed 10 Jun. 2018.

periods[51]. We also need to cover there the rights of the individual to **complain to the ICO**[52], **their right**[53] **to be informed about the personal data we hold about them, their right to object, to access and to rectify or have that data erased. They also have the right**[54] **to restrict data processing and automated decision-making** (eg profiling) as well as the **right**[55] **to take their data elsewhere in a standard electronic or hard copy file format**. This all must be simply and clearly explained.

Experts Recommendations:

Some of the **largest companies have been preparing for GDPR** for years so keep an eye out for how your favourite big brands (eg Google, Microsoft, supermarkets et al) are adjusting their policies as this way **you can get free insights and learning, courtesy of their 'reams' of legal resource!**

---

[51] "GDPR and storage limitation: time to update your data retention policy ...." 22 Jun. 2017,
https://gdpr.report/news/2017/06/22/gdpr-storage-limitation-time-update-data-retention-policy/.
Accessed 10 Jun. 2018.

[52] "Individual rights | ICO."
https://ico.org.uk/for-organisations/guide-to-the-general-data-protection-regulation-gdpr/individual-rights/. Accessed 10 Jun. 2018.

[53] "Chapter 3 – Rights of the data subject | General Data Protection ...." https://gdpr-info.eu/chapter-3/.
Accessed 10 Jun. 2018.

[54] "Chapter 9: Rights of data subjects – Unlocking the EU General Data ...." 13 Sep. 2017,
https://www.whitecase.com/publications/article/chapter-9-rights-data-subjects-unlocking-eu-general-data-protection-regulation. Accessed 10 Jun. 2018.

[55] "Rights of Data Subjects under the GDPR | Law Infographic." 30 Nov. 2017,
https://www.talacka.com/lawinfographic/rights-data-subjects-gdpr/. Accessed 10 Jun. 2018.

This is addressed in Ref: GDPR Articles 5, 6, 12-21[56], 26[57], 28[58] and 29[59].

OK so all that **sounds fine in theory but how do we actually do this in practice**, with multiple colleagues and partners? Below you'll find the **templates I've created for the policies and procedures needed, as well as the reference and evidence documentation required**, to help make this process manageable.

---

[56] "General Data Protection Regulation (GDPR) – Final text neatly arranged." https://gdpr-info.eu/. Accessed 10 Jun. 2018.

[57] "General Data Protection Regulation (GDPR) – Final text neatly arranged." https://gdpr-info.eu/. Accessed 10 Jun. 2018.

[58] "General Data Protection Regulation (GDPR) – Final text neatly arranged." https://gdpr-info.eu/. Accessed 10 Jun. 2018.

[59] "General Data Protection Regulation (GDPR) – Final text neatly arranged." https://gdpr-info.eu/. Accessed 10 Jun. 2018.

Policy	**At Company X Ltd. we acknowledge that providing easy to understand and transparent personal data privacy and consent notices is essential under GDPR and helps us improve our business performance in general.**
	We are committed to ensuring people's personal data is managed competently by us via:
	• Ensuring compliance with all relevant legislation as a minimum.
	• Setting and reviewing performance against objectives and targets that drive continuous improvements in our compliance in this area.
	• Providing sufficient information, resources and training to facilitate the achievement of our objectives in this area.
	Overall responsibility for data privacy and protection in line with GDPR rests with the board of directors. The board of directors discharges this responsibility through the departmental teams who are responsible for the implementation of this Policy. This Policy statement applies to the whole of Company X Ltd.and is available to all employees via our internal file system. Our privacy policy is also made publicly available on our website. The contents of this Policy will be reviewed and updated as necessary and on at least an annual basis.
Procedure	• Annual cycle:
	○ Our Data Privacy & Protection Lead supported by management will review and update our personal data privacy and consent notices annually.
	• Quarterly cycle:
	○ Our Data Privacy & Protection Lead supported by management will update the latest personal data privacy and consent notices on a quarterly basis as needed.
References & Resources	ICO:
	• https://ico.org.uk/for-organisations/guide-to-the-general-data-protection-regulation-gdpr/
	• https://ico.org.uk/media/1624219/preparing-for-the-gdpr-12-steps.pdf
	CIPD:
	• https://www.cipd.co.uk/knowledge/fundamentals/people/hr/policies-factsheet
	SECONDARY:
	Video:
	• https://www.youtube.com/watch?v=xIW5RI8K3Yg
	External Consultant:

	• https://www.linkedin.com/in/mauricebigmoflynn **Book:** • https://www.amazon.co.uk/-/e/B078ZGGLCW

Document Control Reference: GDPR - Issue No: v1.1 - Issue Date: xx/xx/2018 -Review Date: xx/xx/2019

Signature 1: *NAME 1* - Data Privacy & Protection Lead

Signature 2: *NAME 2* - Director

Company X Ltd., ADDRESS, UK +44 (0)TELEPHONE NUMBER.

Privacy Notice Example	You can contact us at: Company X Ltd., ADDRESS, UK +44 (0)TELEPHONE NUMBER, Email. We have personal data from the following: Clients Business Contacts Employees & Directors Other Website Visitors Other? We process your personal data in X ways. 1. Website data analysis - we use the following types of personal data for this: xyz. We store this data in the following countries: xyz. We retain this data for x months. The legal reason we can do this is called legitimate interests/existing contract/consent/other law/other. Our legitimate interests/existing contract/consent/other law/other justification/evidence is: xyz. We get this data from yourself. The only third parties we might share this data with are xyz. 2. Website services provision - we use the following types of personal data for this:xyz. We store this data in the following countries: xyz. We retain this data for x months. The legal reason we can do this is called legitimate interests/existing contract/consent/other law/other. Our legitimate interests/existing contract/consent/other law/other justification/evidence is: xyz.. We get this data from yourself. The only third parties we might share this data with are xyz. 3. Business communications - we use the following types of personal data for this: xyz. We store this data in the following countries: xyz. We retain this data for x months. The legal reason we can do this is called legitimate interests. Our legitimate interests/existing contract/consent/other law/other justification/evidence is: xyz.We get this data from yourself. The only third parties we might share this data with are xyz. 4. Other? You have qualified rights to access, rectify, and erase your personal data; and to restrict or object to processing; and to make your data portable + LINKS. You have the right to complain to a Supervisory Authority + LINK.
Consent Text Example	Welcome - in order to give you access to our service xyz at Company X Ltd.we need to use the following personal information of yours (eg name, email, phone number, company name, other) in order to do xyz. Please therefore take a moment to read our Privacy Notice via the link below and confirm your consent by ticking the box next to "I consent" or clicking the button "I consent."
Legitimate Interest Text Example	To give you access to the services that you are requesting, we of course need to use the personal information that you provide on this form. We always keep your personal information safe and secure, so please take a minute to read our latest Privacy Notice via this link on our website + LINK, which tells you everything you need to know about your rights relating to your personal data. That way when you submit this form to us, this will confirm to us that you have read and accept our Privacy Policy, which is all about how we protect your personal data and privacy.

Verbal Consent Notice (If Needed)	Of course we'll need to use your personal information that you've given - such as your email etc - in order to provide you with the services that you've asked for. Please can you therefore take a moment to read our latest Privacy Notice from the link we have provided (in our confirmation email/on our website + LINK), which gives more information on this.

Document Control Reference: GDPR - Issue No: v1.1 - Issue Date: xx/xx/2018 -Review Date: xx/xx/2019

Signature 1: *NAME 1* - Data Privacy & Protection Lead

Signature 2: *NAME 2* - Director

Company X Ltd., ADDRESS, UK +44 (0)TELEPHONE NUMBER.

OK that's clear! Where do we go next?

1.7 Data (subject access) requests

How many requests?

Companies using personal data need to be ready to **respond at short notice** to data requests[60] from

---

[60] "How to request your personal data under GDPR - TechRepublic." 24 Apr. 2018, https://www.techrepublic.com/article/how-to-request-your-personal-data-under-gdpr/. Accessed 10 Jun. 2018.

individuals. Most companies **do not have the resources** or tools to do this reliably and **penalties for failure are potentially high**. We need to first understand the new requirements and put in place the **people, processes and tools** to ensure compliance. All **employees and data sharing partners will need to get training** about the new requirements and processes to avoid risk of human error. The jargon for these is Subject Access Requests or SARs for short.

I thee request ...

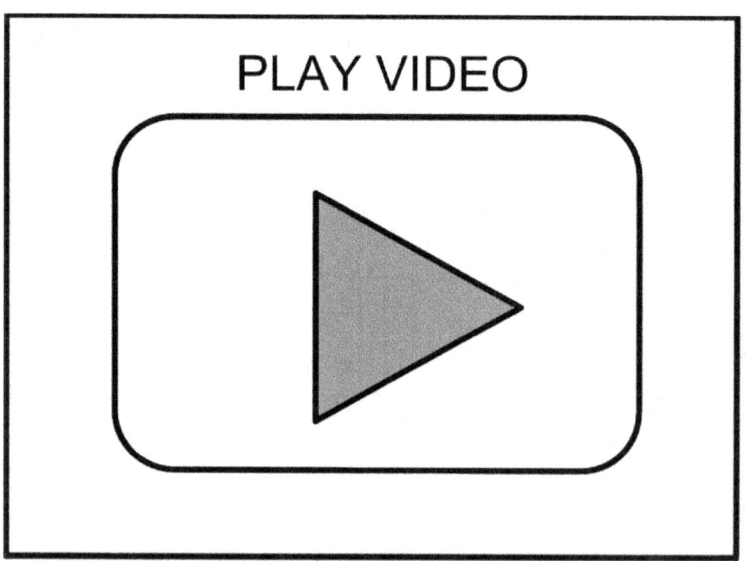

[VIDEO: https://www.youtube.com/watch?v=Ezdxq4vgAio]

Data requests from individuals can relate to any of the **rights[61] mentioned in the above step i.e. rights to object, be informed, to access, to rectify, to erase, to restrict (1on1) processing and automated decision-making plus the right for personal data portability.** Companies have **one month to respond[62]** and **cannot charge** for these data requests, unless excessive. **If a company refuses**, it must **communicate why as well as the right for the individual to complain** for independent judgement i.e. via the ICO.

What the experts say:

Responding to data requests is essential but few companies have the processes in place to comply reliably. **It's also hard to anticipate how many we might receive.** Smaller companies are therefore tending to **set up semi-manual processes for this** at least until the size of potential demand is clearer. Larger companies look to use **semi automated software tools** as far as possible, as probably the best scalable solution to use, especially when trying to **find all the records in big data sets held in multiple places**.

---

[61] "Chapter 3 – Rights of the data subject | General Data Protection ...." https://gdpr-info.eu/chapter-3/. Accessed 10 Jun. 2018.
[62] "GDPR Subject Access Requests - GDPR.Report." 20 Nov. 2017, https://gdpr.report/news/2017/11/20/gdpr-subject-access-requests/. Accessed 10 Jun. 2018.

This is addressed in GDPR Articles 6,12,15-22[63].

OK so all that **sounds fine in theory but how do we actually do this in practice**, with multiple colleagues and partners? Below you'll find the **templates I've created for the policies and procedures needed, as well as the reference and evidence documentation required**, to help make this process manageable.

---

[63] "General Data Protection Regulation (GDPR) – Final text neatly arranged." https://gdpr-info.eu/. Accessed 10 Jun. 2018.

Policy	**At Company X Ltd. we acknowledge that organising an easy to understand personal data request procedure (also known as SAR Subject Access Record request) for is essential under GDPR and helps us improve our business performance in general.** We are committed to ensuring people's personal data is managed competently by us via: • Ensuring compliance with all relevant legislation as a minimum. • Setting and reviewing performance against objectives and targets that drive continuous improvements in our compliance in this area. • Providing sufficient information, resources and training to facilitate the achievement of our objectives in this area. Overall responsibility for data privacy and protection in line with GDPR rests with the board of directors. The board of directors discharges this responsibility through the departmental teams who are responsible for the implementation of this Policy. This Policy statement applies to the whole of Company X Ltd.and is available to all employees via our internal file system. Our privacy policy is also made publicly available on our website. The contents of this Policy will be reviewed and updated as necessary and on at least an annual basis.

Procedure	• **All personal data requests and enquiries to be forwarded to Data Privacy & Protection Lead - All Staff**
	• **Week 1: Authenticate ID & clarify/confirm request plus identify data controllers and processors - Data Privacy & Protection Lead**
	
	NB:
	
	• **Data controllers lead & data processors follow their instructions**
	• **Controllers = gathered the data and/or set the terms of the privacy policy**
	
	• **Weeks 2/3: Complete internal procedures:**
	    ○ **Electronic searches** - IT, HR, Finance, Marketing, Sales, Other
	    ○ **Manual searches** - IT, HR, Finance, Marketing, Sales, Other
	    ○ **Recommend data to Inform/Rectify/Erase/Port/Opt Out** - IT, HR, Finance, Marketing, Sales, Other
	        ■ **Inform**: List of data we have, what we use if for & how long, who we share it with.
	        ■ **Object/Rectify/Erase/Access/Port:** Where is the data stored?
	        ■ **Opt out of profiling:** Where do we record opt outs?
	    ○ **Collate hardcopy or electronic file (CSV and/or pdf file) - Data Privacy & Protection Lead**
	• **Week 4: Complete & confirm procedure (or request extension) - Data Privacy & Protection Lead**

References & Resources	**PRIMARY:** **ICO:** - https://ico.org.uk/for-organisations/guide-to-the-general-data-protection-regulation-gdpr/ - https://ico.org.uk/media/1624219/preparing-for-the-gdpr-12-steps.pdf **CIPD:** - https://www.cipd.co.uk/knowledge/fundamentals/people/hr/policies-factsheet **SECONDARY:** **External Consultant:** - https://www.linkedin.com/in/mauricebigmoflynn **Book:** - https://www.amazon.co.uk/-/e/B078ZGGLCW

Message Templates	**RECEIPT COMMUNICATION:**
	--------------------------------- 	
	Dear Sir/Madam,
	Thank you for your recent message regarding your personal data.
	Please could you confirm the following in writing:
	- That you are NAME and can provide documentary evidence eg passport photocopy (to be attached).
	- That you want us to do the following:
	    - (If requested) Inform you of the personal data we have for you, what we use it for & for how long and who if anyone we share it with.
	    - (If requested) Rectify your personal data as follows "xyz."
	    - (If requested) Erase your personal data from our systems (if not required for legal reasons).
	    - (If requested) Send you your personal data in a convenient file format. Please indicate preferred file format: 1. pdf 2. CSV 3. other.
	    - (If requested) Opt you out of individualised personal profiling and automated decision making.
	
	We aim to complete this within 30 days as required and will keep you informed re our progress.
	
	Kind regards etc.
	
	--------------------------------------- 	

COMPLETION COMMUNICATION:

Dear Sir/Madam,

Thank you for your recent message regarding your personal data.

We are pleased to confirm completion of the task you requested ie

- (If requested) Inform you of the personal data we have for you, what we use it for & for how long and who if anyone we share it with. Please find that information in the report included here.
- (If requested) Rectify your personal data as follows "xyz."
- (If requested) Erase your personal data from our systems (if not required for legal reasons).
- (If requested) Send you your personal data in a convenient file format. Please find that information in the file included here.
- (If requested) Opt you out of individualised personal profiling and automated decision making.

Kind regards etc.

SAR REPORT FOR MANAGEMENT:

Dear Management Team,

As part of our GDPR compliance reporting procedure, here are the statistics for the last x months for data requests (SAR) received and fulfilled:

No. of requests: x

% Fulfilled within 30 days: xx%

% Fulfilled within extended time up to 90 days: xx%

% Not fulfilled within deadline: xx%

Reason for any fails: xyz

Actions undertaken to remedy: xyz

Kind regards etc.

Document Control Reference: GDPR - Issue No: v1.1 - Issue Date: xx/xx/2018 -Review Date: xx/xx/2019

Signature 1: *NAME 1* - Data Privacy & Protection Lead

Signature 2:   *NAME 2*   - Director

Company X Ltd., ADDRESS, UK +44 (0)TELEPHONE NUMBER.

OK got it! So what's next?

1.8 Data breach process

Breach breach!

Until now companies have often **kept quiet about data breaches, hacks and leaks** - as there was little incentive to go public - but that's all changing. We now need to

report personal data breaches[64] **very quickly or risk big fines**. Most companies recognise they don't currently have the people, processes or tools to do this scalably. We need to first understand **what is required** under GDPR and put in place the **people, processes and tools** to ensure compliance. All **employees and data sharing partners will need to understand** the new requirements, to avoid the risk of human error.

Under attack!

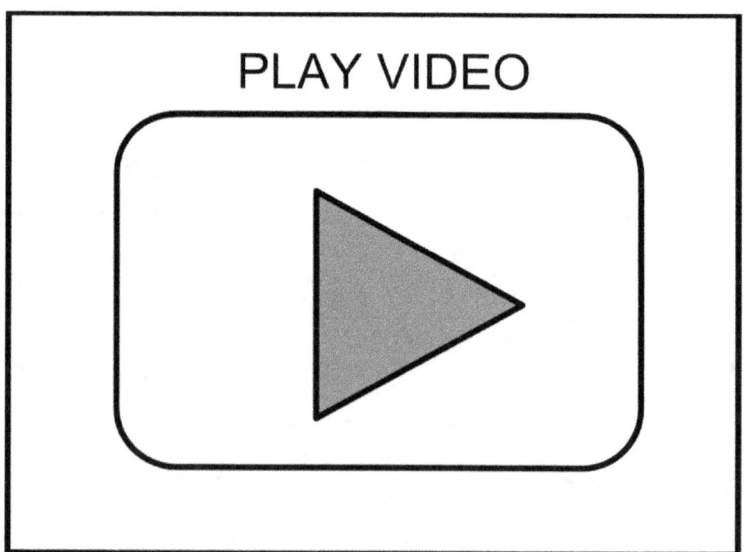

[VIDEO: https://www.youtube.com/watch?v=PToCYQ-cxwk]

Personal data breaches which might cause financial or reputational damage to the individual, must be reported

---

[64] "Art. 33 GDPR – Notification of a personal data breach to the ...." https://gdpr-info.eu/art-33-gdpr/. Accessed 10 Jun. 2018.

to the Information Commissioner's Office ([ico.org.uk](ico.org.uk)) **within 72 hours**[65] - or else we risk fines of up to 20m Euros or 4% global turnover, whichever is larger! Data breaches must also be reported to the individuals involved without delay[66] **if high risk of damaging the individual and their rights e.g. via discrimination, reputational damage, financial loss, loss of confidentiality or any other significant economic or social disadvantage.**

Even when we don't need to inform the ICO it's **good practice to record breaches and near-breaches internally** so we can learn from them and anticipate future issues. The ICO is now also encouraging us to **test these key processes in advance, through drills and practices.**

What the experts say:

Imagine trying to deal manually with a data breach at **midnight on 25th December** or other big national holidays! Smaller companies are tending to **set up semi-manual processes** to prepare to respond effectively. Larger companies are looking to use **semi**

---

[65] "Art. 33 GDPR – Notification of a personal data breach to the ...." https://gdpr-info.eu/art-33-gdpr/. Accessed 10 Jun. 2018.

[66] "Art. 33 GDPR – Notification of a personal data breach to the ...." https://gdpr-info.eu/art-33-gdpr/. Accessed 10 Jun. 2018.

automated software tools as probably the best scalable solution.

This is addressed in GDPR Article 12 and 33[67].

OK so all that **sounds fine in theory but how do we actually do this in practice**, with multiple colleagues and partners? Below you'll find the **templates I've created for the policies and procedures needed, as well as the reference and evidence documentation required**, to help make this process manageable.

[67] "General Data Protection Regulation (GDPR) – Final text neatly arranged." https://gdpr-info.eu/. Accessed 10 Jun. 2018.

Policy	At Company X Ltd. we acknowledge that organising an easy to understand personal data breach response procedure is essential under GDPR and helps us improve our business performance in general.
	
	We are committed to ensuring people's personal data is managed competently by us via:
	    • Ensuring compliance with all relevant legislation as a minimum.
	    • Setting and reviewing performance against objectives and targets that drive continuous improvements in our compliance in this area.
	    • Providing sufficient information, resources and training to facilitate the achievement of our objectives in this area.
	
	Overall responsibility for data privacy and protection in line with GDPR rests with the board of directors. The board of directors discharges this responsibility through the departmental teams who are responsible for the implementation of this Policy. This Policy statement applies to the whole of Company X Ltd.and is available to all employees via our internal file system. Our privacy policy is also made publicly available on our website. The contents of this Policy will be reviewed and updated as necessary and on at least an annual basis.

Procedure	• <u>All personal data breach issues, near misses and related concerns (ie leaks or deletion) to be reported ASAP to Data Privacy & Protection Lead - All Staff</u>
	• <u>Day 1: Verify, fix breach & assess risk level</u> - **Data Privacy & Protection Lead with relevant department (IT/Finance/HR/Sales/Marketing/Other)**
	
	NB Risk Assessment: A breach or near miss involving ...
	
	1. Personal data with low risk of financial or reputational risk => report internally
	2. Personal data with risk of financial or reputational risk => report to ICO
	3. Personal data with high unmitigated risk of financial or reputational risk => report to data subjects without undue delay
	
	• <u>Day 2: Prepare documentation</u> - **Data Privacy & Protection Lead with relevant department (IT/Finance/HR/Sales/Marketing/Other)**
	    ○ Internal Report (template below)
	    ○ ICO Report (if required - (template below)
	    ○ Data Subject Report (if required - template below)
	• <u>Day 3: Complete Procedure:</u> - **GDPR Project Lead**

References & Resources	<u>PRIMARY:</u>
	
	ICO:
	
	    • https://ico.org.uk/for-organisations/guide-to-the-general-data-protection-regulation-gdpr/
	    • https://ico.org.uk/media/1624219/preparing-for-the-gdpr-12-steps.pdf

CIPD:

- https://www.cipd.co.uk/knowledge/fundamentals/people/hr/policies-factsheet

SECONDARY:

External Consultant:

- https://www.linkedin.com/in/mauricebigmoflynn

Books:

- https://www.amazon.co.uk/-/e/B078ZGGLCW

Document Control Reference: GDPR - Issue No: v1.1 - Issue Date: xx/xx/2018 -Review Date: xx/xx/2019

Signature 1: *NAME 1* - Data Privacy & Protection Lead

Signature 2: *NAME 2* - Director

Company X Ltd., ADDRESS, UK +44 (0)TELEPHONE NUMBER.

DATA BREACH OR NEAR MISS REPORT:	DETAILS:
Name of organisation?	
Data privacy and protection lead?	Name: Job Title: Email: Phone Number: Address:
When did this breach occur? (If unknown, please provide an approximate date)	xx/xx/20xx
When was the breach initially detected?	xx/xx/20xx
Briefly describe the breach?	(eg theft, loss, copying)
What is the nature and content of the personal data involved?	
What technical and organisational security measures have you applied to the affected personal data?	Eg lost mobile phone has been wiped remotely of data
Were other companies involved?	
Summarise the incident that caused the breach?	
What was the physical location of the breach and the storage media type?	Eg electronic files, hard copies
How many individuals were affected?	
What are the potential consequences and adverse effects on those individuals?	Eg financial, reputational, ID fraud, other

What technical and organisational measures have you taken to mitigate those potential adverse effects?	
How were customers notified?	Eg by email
Please provide the content of any notification to customers?	
How many customers were notified?	
Does the breach affect individuals in other EU member states?	If so, which countries?
Have you notified any other data protection authorities?	if so, which ones?
Solutions identified to prevent such breaches in future?	
Other safeguards, security measures and mechanisms to ensure compliance in future?	
Cumulative breach summary	Breaches this year: xx Breaches last year: xx YoY %: xx Brief summary of causes: Brief summary of solutions:

Document Control Reference: GDPR - Issue No: v1.1 - Issue Date: xx/xx/2018 -Review Date: xx/xx/2019

Signature 1: *NAME 1* - Data Privacy & Protection Lead

Signature 2: *NAME 2* - Director

Company X Ltd., ADDRESS, UK +44 (0)TELEPHONE NUMBER.1`

Still with it? OK, on to the next!

1.9 Worldwide data transfers

Planning for the international space?

Personal data transfers to **countries outside the EU and a short list of approved countries is restricted**[68].

---

[68] "Top 10 operational impacts of the GDPR: Part 4 - Cross-border data ...."
https://iapp.org/news/a/top-10-operational-impacts-of-the-gdpr-part-4-cross-border-data-transfers/.
Accessed 10 Jun. 2018.

The EU's governing bodies **want to deal with local contacts** wherever possible when it comes to issues of GDPR compliance, so companies have to select and document where their data decisions are taken (called your **"lead data protection supervisory authority**[69].")

Around the world?

Your lead data protection supervisory authority is your supervisory authority **in the state where your main establishment is.** Your main establishment is your **EU central administration and the location where data decisions are made.** Personal data transfers between countries and outside the EU **must be made under certain secure, approved processes only**[70].

Expert Recommendation:

For UK led companies your lead office will be **UK HQ until after Brexit.** For European, non UK led companies this will be the **European HQ** most of the time, unless local factors intervene. **Data transfer rules** are still under debate in some areas - see below.

---

[69] "International transfers | ICO."
https://ico.org.uk/for-organisations/guide-to-the-general-data-protection-regulation-gdpr/international-transfers/. Accessed 10 Jun. 2018.
[70] "privacy shield and data transfers under the gdpr." 25 May. 2018,
https://files.alston.com/files/docs/Roadmap-to-the-GDPR-International-Data-Transfers.pdf. Accessed 10 Jun. 2018.

This is addressed in GDPR Articles 27 and 45-49[71].

OK so all that **sounds fine in theory but how do we actually do this in practice**, with multiple colleagues and partners? Below you'll find the **templates I've created for the policies and procedures needed, as well as the reference and evidence documentation required**, to help make this process manageable.

[71] "General Data Protection Regulation (GDPR) – Final text neatly arranged." https://gdpr-info.eu/. Accessed 10 Jun. 2018.

Step 10: Guides & documentation

Policy	**At Company X Ltd. we acknowledge that ensuring a clear understanding of personal data transfer rules including international under GDPR is essential across the business and helps us improve our business performance in general.** We are committed to ensuring people's personal data is managed competently by us via: • Ensuring compliance with all relevant legislation as a minimum. • Setting and reviewing performance against objectives and targets that drive continuous improvements in our compliance in this area. • Providing sufficient information, resources and training to facilitate the achievement of our objectives in this area. Overall responsibility for data privacy and protection in line with GDPR rests with the board of directors. The board of directors discharges this responsibility through the departmental teams who are responsible for the implementation of this Policy. This Policy statement applies to the whole of Company X Ltd.and is available to all employees via our internal file system. Our privacy policy is also made publicly available on our website. The contents of this Policy will be reviewed and updated as necessary and on at least an annual basis.
Procedure	1. Personal data transfer with another office in the same company in the UK = Allowed if company has policies and procedures in place to ensure GDPR compliance. 2. Personal data transfer with another organisation in the UK = Allowed if the companies have a GDPR compliant data protection agreement in place - see template below. 3. Personal data transfer within EU/EEA = Allowed as long as 1 or 2 above applies. 4. Personal data transfer with to country on EU list for having adequate personal data protection laws (see below) = Allowed as long as 1 or 2 above applies. NB EU list of countries with adequate personal data protection laws: Andorra, Argentina, Canada (commercial organisations), Faroe Islands, Guernsey, Israel, Isle of Man, Jersey, New Zealand, Switzerland, Uruguay and the US (limited to the Privacy Shield framework). Adequacy talks are ongoing with Japan and South Korea. 5. Personal data transfer with US or Switzerland = Allowed under EU-US-SW Privacy Shield Certification. 6. Passenger name records PNR for air travel = Allowed for US/Canada/Australia (via bilateral agreement). 7. For personal data transfer with an office in your organisation in another country not on the approved lists above = Only allowed if "Binding Corporate Rules" have been approved by the ICO or equivalent. 8. For personal data transfer with another organisation in another country not on the approved lists above = Only allowed if recommended "model contract clauses"(see below) are added to the partner contract and a risk assessment is made re potential GDPR compliance issues.

References & Resources	PRIMARY:
	
	ICO:
	
	   • https://ico.org.uk/for-organisations/guide-to-the-general-data-protection-regulation-gdpr/
	   • https://ico.org.uk/media/1624219/preparing-for-the-gdpr-12-steps.pdf
	
	EU:
	
	   • https://ec.europa.eu/info/law/law-topic/data-protection/data-transfers-outside-eu_en
	
	Data Protection - Processor Terms:
	
	   • https://www.dlapiper.com/en/uk/insights/publications/2017/08/example-gdpr-ready-processor-terms/
	
	CIPD:
	
	   • https://www.cipd.co.uk/knowledge/fundamentals/people/hr/policies-factsheet
	
	SECONDARY:
	
	Book:
	
	   • https://www.amazon.co.uk/-/e/B078ZGGLCW

Document Control Reference: GDPR - Issue No: v1.1 - Issue Date: xx/xx/2018 -Review Date: xx/xx/2019

Signature 1: *NAME 1* - Data Privacy & Protection Lead

Signature 2: *NAME 2* - Director

Company X Ltd., ADDRESS, UK +44 (0)TELEPHONE NUMBER.

Still with it! Let's see what's next?

1.10 Sensitive (special category) data and kids

Feeling sensitive?

As you might expect **childrens[72]' and other sensitive data[73] merits extra protection,** although it **varies by country.** The main issue for kids is **from whom the consent permission needs to come** from and **from what age are they legally responsible for their own data decisions**? For sensitive data (e.g. race/ethnic origins, politics, religion, trade union status, health, sex preference, criminal record), we can **only use it in restricted ways i.e. via consent or existing law and only in agreed and proscribed ways**. Sensitive data has also been extended under GDPR to include genetic data and biometric data. We clearly need to understand **what consent for children means under GDPR and audit our data accordingly.** We also need to be clear on **how other sensitive data can be used**. Compliant data can be used for the **permitted ways and time periods. Non compliant data must be deleted or re-checked eg for permission or another lawful basis.**

How old are you?

In the UK under GDPR children can give their own consent to personal data usage **at 13 years and above**. Other countries will set the age limit **between 13-16 years**. Under these age limits consent must be obtained

---

[72] "Art. 8 GDPR – Conditions applicable to child's consent in relation to ...."
https://gdpr-info.eu/art-8-gdpr/. Accessed 10 Jun. 2018.
[73] "Art. 9 GDPR – Processing of special categories of personal data ...." https://gdpr-info.eu/art-9-gdpr/.
Accessed 10 Jun. 2018.

from the **parent or legal guardian**. Sensitive data use (e.g. health, ethnicity, criminal records et al) **must comply with all existing restrictions (e.g. minimised use for legally defined and permitted tasks) with added transparency required under GDPR. Public bodies cannot rely on "legitimate interest." Criminal record data checking needs to be done via approved organisations.**

What the experts say:

One of the key challenges here is the **different treatment of children by age of consent across countries.** For sensitive data **specialist advice is recommended if this is a big part of the business model.**

This is addressed in GDPR Articles 8, 9 and 10[74].

OK so all that **sounds fine in theory but how do we actually do this in practice**, with multiple colleagues and partners? Below you'll find the **templates I've created for the policies and procedures needed, as well as the reference and evidence documentation required**, to help make this process manageable.

---

[74] "General Data Protection Regulation (GDPR) – Final text neatly arranged." https://gdpr-info.eu/. Accessed 10 Jun. 2018.

Policy	At Company X Ltd. we acknowledge that ensuring a clear understanding of special category (sensitive) and kids personal data usage rules across the business is essential under GDPR and helps us improve our business performance in general. We are committed to ensuring people's personal data is managed competently by us via: • Ensuring compliance with all relevant legislation as a minimum. • Setting and reviewing performance against objectives and targets that drive continuous improvements in our compliance in this area. • Providing sufficient information, resources and training to facilitate the achievement of our objectives in this area. Overall responsibility for data privacy and protection in line with GDPR rests with the board of directors. The board of directors discharges this responsibility through the departmental teams who are responsible for the implementation of this Policy. This Policy statement applies to the whole of Company X Ltd.and is available to all employees via our internal file system. Our privacy policy is also made publicly available on our website. The contents of this Policy will be reviewed and updated as necessary and on at least an annual basis.

Procedure	• Annual cycle:
	   ○ We summarise our use and protection of special category (sensitive) data and children's data (if relevant) in our data & risk audit in Step 2 above.
	   ○ Our Data Privacy & Protection Lead supported by management will annually review and revise our plans for use of any childrens' and special category (sensitive) personal data types according to latest direction from the ICO.
	• Quarterly cycle:
	   ○ We summarise our use and protection of special category (sensitive) data and children's data (if relevant) in our data & risk audit in Step 2 above.
	   ○ Our Data Privacy & Protection Lead supported by management will review and revise quarterly our plans for use of any children's(if relevant) and special category (sensitive) personal data types according to latest direction from the ICO.

References & Resources	PRIMARY: ICO: • https://ico.org.uk/for-organisations/guide-to-the-general-data-protection-regulation-gdpr/ • https://ico.org.uk/for-organisations/guide-to-the-general-data-protection-regulation-gdpr/lawful-basis-for-Procedureing/special-category-data

87

- https://ico.org.uk/media/1624219/preparing-for-the-gdpr-12-steps.pdf

CIPD:

- https://www.cipd.co.uk/knowledge/fundamentals/people/hr/policies-factsheet

SECONDARY:

External Consultant:

- https://www.linkedin.com/in/mauricebigmoflynn

Book:

- https://www.amazon.co.uk/-/e/B078ZGGLCW

Document Control Reference: GDPR - Issue No: v1.1 - Issue Date: xx/xx/2018 -Review Date: xx/xx/2019

Signature 1: *NAME 1* - Data Privacy & Protection Lead

Signature 2: *NAME 2* - Director

Company X Ltd., ADDRESS, UK +44 (0)TELEPHONE NUMBER.

Last step! Let's see what's next?

1.11 Privacy and protection by design

By design and default?

Many companies have had as many data leakage risks as an old watering can has water leaks! **Employees roam the world accessing and sharing personal data on**

a variety of devices and systems only some of which are secure. GDPR means this cannot continue. A better approach means **rethinking personal data usage** in your company and **ensuring it cannot leak, by design**[75] rather than leaving to chance. Most companies recognise they don't currently have the people, processes or tools **to do this scalably**. We need to first understand **what is required** under GDPR and put in place the **people, processes and tools** to ensure compliance.

By default?

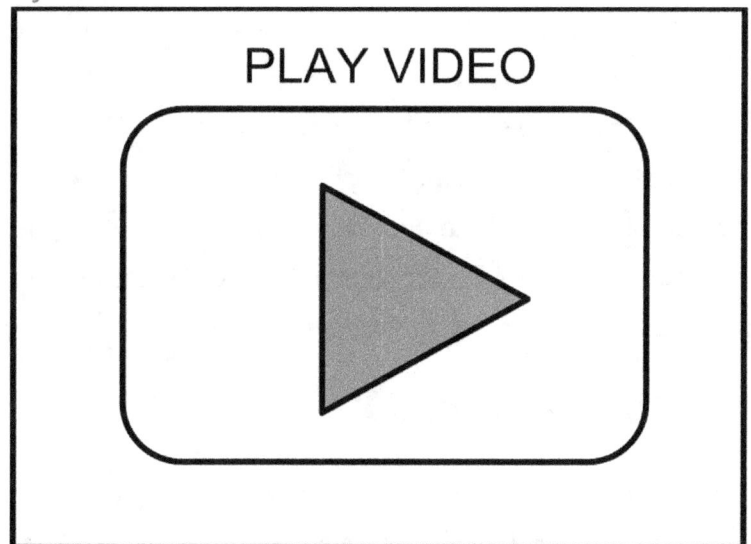

[VIDEO:
https://www.oracle.com/uk/corporate/features/gdpr.html?bcid=5584974298001&playerType=single-social&size=w01&shareUrl=http://www.oracle.com#close]

---

[75] "Art. 25 GDPR – Data protection by design and by default | General ...." https://gdpr-info.eu/art-25-gdpr/. Accessed 10 Jun. 2018.

Protection and privacy by design and by default means building privacy into every process and system **from the ground up** and from scratch when needed. We can **map the flows of data** and **cut out areas of risk** e.g. human error. To get there we need to **minimise & delete old data, protect, anonymised, pseudonymise & encrypt our current data plus inform and give access to the data for data subjects on request**.

Also introducing **Data Protection Impact Assessments**[76] which are for new, high risk areas e.g. big data transfers, between old and new systems. For most companies this is an internal process. For companies with a **DPO, the ICO can review DPIA's** and provide feedback. **Within 8 weeks of submitting a DPIA** (plus an additional 6 weeks for complex cases), the supervisory authority (i.e. in the UK this is the ICO) **will give advice on whether the intended project has large GDPR risk issues.**

What the experts say:

For big companies with large amounts of data **this represents a big set of changes and requirements.** For smaller companies **the requirements are much less onerous.**

---

[76] "Art. 35 GDPR – Data protection impact assessment | General Data ...."
https://gdpr-info.eu/art-35-gdpr/. Accessed 10 Jun. 2018.

This is addressed in GDPR Articles 5, 24, 25 and 32[77].

OK so all that **sounds fine in theory but how do we actually do this in practice**, with multiple colleagues and partners? Below you'll find the **templates I've created for the policies and procedures needed, as well as the reference and evidence documentation required**, to help make this process manageable.

---

[77] "General Data Protection Regulation (GDPR) – Final text neatly arranged." https://gdpr-info.eu/. Accessed 10 Jun. 2018.

Policy	**At Company X Ltd. we acknowledge that data protection and privacy by design and default is essential under GDPR and helps us improve our business performance in general.** We are committed to ensuring people's personal data is managed competently by us via: • Ensuring compliance with all relevant legislation as a minimum. • Setting and reviewing performance against objectives and targets that drive continuous improvements in our compliance in this area. • Providing sufficient information, resources and training to facilitate the achievement of our objectives in this area. Overall responsibility for data privacy and protection in line with GDPR rests with the board of directors. The board of directors discharges this responsibility through the departmental teams who are responsible for the implementation of this Policy. This Policy statement applies to the whole of Company X Ltd.and is available to all employees via our internal file system. Our privacy policy is also made publicly available on our website. The contents of this Policy will be reviewed and updated as necessary and on at least an annual basis.

Procedure	• <u>Annual cycle</u>:
	    o We summarise our approach to personal data privacy and protection by design and default in our audit report below.
	    o Our Data Privacy & Protection Lead supported by management will annually review and revise our plans for personal data privacy and protection by design and default according to latest direction from the ICO.
	
	• <u>Quarterly cycle</u>:
	    o We summarise our approach to personal data privacy and protection by design and default in our audit report below.
	    o Our Data Privacy & Protection Lead supported by management will review and revise on a quarterly basis our plans for personal data privacy and protection by design and default according to latest direction from the ICO.

Resources	<u>**PRIMARY:**</u> **ICO:** • https://ico.org.uk/for-organisations/guide-to-the-general-data-protection-regulation-gdpr/ • https://ico.org.uk/media/1624219/preparing-for-the-gdpr-12-steps.pdf

94

CIPD:

- https://www.cipd.co.uk/knowledge/fundamentals/people/hr/policies-factsheet

SECONDARY:

External Consultant:

- https://www.linkedin.com/in/mauricebigmoflynn

Book:

- https://www.amazon.co.uk/-/e/B078ZGGLCW

Document Control Reference: GDPR - Issue No: v1.1 - Issue Date: xx/xx/2018 -Review Date: xx/xx/2019

Signature 1: *NAME 1* - Data Privacy & Protection Lead

Signature 2: *NAME 2* - Director

Company X Ltd., ADDRESS, UK +44 (0)TELEPHONE NUMBER.

Step 11: Guides & documentation

NB For SMEs with small non sensitive data sets then an awareness of this topic and progress as outlined in the 12 steps here plus a "common sense" approach should suffice. Higher importance elements are underlined below.	
InfoSec policy eg via ISO27001	YES/NO
Data classification procedure	YES/NO
Encryption procedure (for data on the move)	YES/NO
Identity Access Management (need to know basis)	YES/NO
Software tools for aggregation, data masking, pseudonymisation, and anonymisation	YES/NO
Enterprise privacy risk assessment and mitigation plan	YES/NO
Whistleblower procedure	YES/NO
Audits of methodology	YES/NO
Record retention policy	YES/NO
Project security risk assessments	YES/NO
Perimeter security measures	YES/NO
System monitoring	YES/NO
Acceptable use policy	YES/NO
Password parameters	YES/NO
Data center security measures (e.g., biometrics, access restriction, monitoring)	YES/NO
Electronic badge access system - physical records cupboards locked	YES/NO
Clean desk policy	YES/NO
Employee agreement outlines security responsibilities	YES/NO
Employee termination checklist	YES/NO
Employee background checks	YES/NO
Data loss prevention (DLP) software	YES/NO

Data privacy and security requirements for third parties	YES/NO
Contracts with third parties for data sharing	YES/NO
Business continuity plan	YES/NO
Job descriptions for data protection-related roles	YES/NO
Defined privacy roles and responsibilities	YES/NO
Data protection training and awareness materials	YES/NO
Data protection as a regular agenda item for the board	YES/NO
Data protection impact assessment templates	YES/NO
Data protection impact assessment guidelines	YES/NO
Policy on conflict of interests	YES/NO
Formal reporting structures	YES/NO
Procedures for handling inquiries and complaints	YES/NO
Data privacy notice	YES/NO
Document control procedure GDPR	YES/NO
Data Protection Policy Review Procedure GDPR	YES/NO
Responding to Information Security Reports procedure	YES/NO
Information security event reports	YES/NO

Document Control Reference: GDPR - Issue No: v1.1 - Issue Date: xx/xx/2018 -Review Date: xx/xx/2019

Signature 1:   *NAME 1*   - Data Privacy & Protection Lead

Signature 2:   *NAME 2*   - Director

Company X Ltd., ADDRESS, UK +44 (0)TELEPHONE NUMBER.

Step 11: Guides & documentation

Data protection impact assessment process (DPIA)

NB To be completed for all projects with major personal data breach risks eg major platform changes Questions?	Answers?
What is the aim and description of the project?	
What personal data will be collected?	
How will the personal data be collected?	
Where will the personal data be stored?	
Where will the personal data be shared?	
How will the personal data be amended or deleted?	
GDPR risks identified (individual, organisational, compliance)?	
Solutions identified (individual, organisational, compliance)?	
Other safeguards, security measures and mechanisms to ensure compliance?	

Document Control Reference: GDPR - Issue No: v1.1 - Issue Date: xx/xx/2018 -Review Date: xx/xx/2019

Signature 1: *NAME 1*   - Data Privacy & Protection Lead

Signature 2: *NAME 2* - Director

Company X Ltd., ADDRESS, UK +44 (0)TELEPHONE NUMBER.

Last step! Let's see what's next?

1.12 Project plan

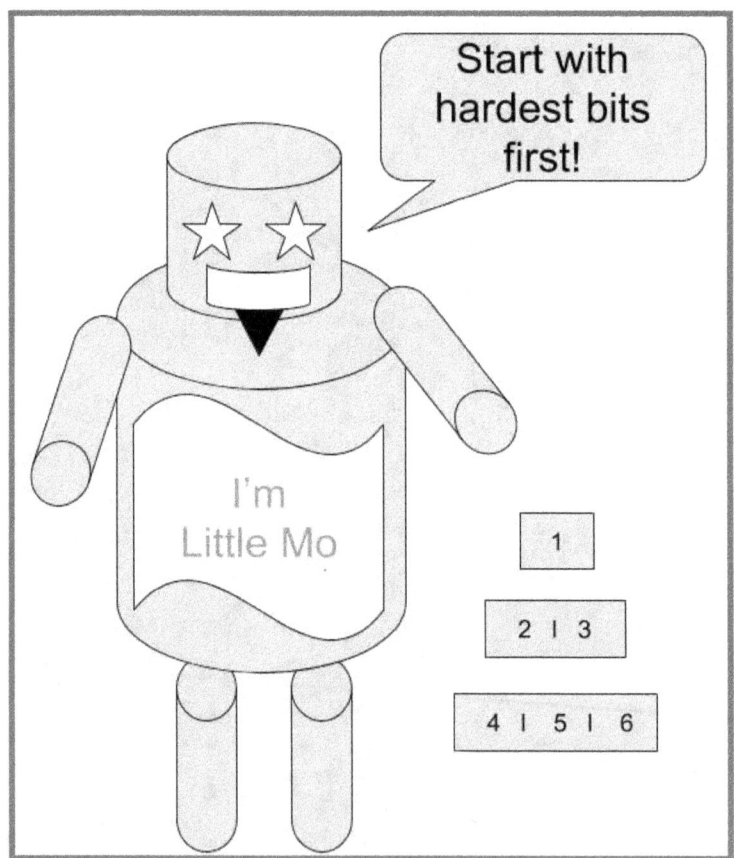

Project plans?

Big companies have been preparing for GDPR for years but some **smaller companies** still haven't started. We all need to **start now and focus on the priorities.**

Let's Prioritise!

The key elements for **attacking GDPR prep with speed and prioritisation**, are generally agreed to be the following:

1. A cross functional Data Privacy Steering Committee with a board level sponsor and expert external partners if needed;

2. The data audit with risk, gap and data flow analysis;

3. The project timeline, with resources and critical path;

4. Our data protection and privacy policy i.e. summarising all the 12 steps we're taking, fully tailored for the business.

What the experts say?

This does not have to be too difficult if you **start today & prioritise!**

OK so all that **sounds fine in theory but how do we actually do this in practice**, with multiple colleagues and partners? Below you'll find the **templates I've created for the policies and procedures needed, as well as the reference and evidence documentation required**, to help make this process manageable.

Policy	**At Company X Ltd. we acknowledge that having a clear project plan and critical path is essential for GDPR prep and helps us improve our business performance in general.** We are committed to ensuring people's personal data is managed competently by us via: • Ensuring compliance with all relevant legislation as a minimum. • Setting and reviewing performance against objectives and targets that drive continuous improvements in our compliance in this area. • Providing sufficient information, resources and training to facilitate the achievement of our objectives in this area. Overall responsibility for data privacy and protection in line with GDPR rests with the board of directors. The board of directors discharges this responsibility through the departmental teams who are responsible for the implementation of this Policy. This Policy statement applies to the whole of Company X Ltd.and is available to all employees via our internal file system. Our privacy policy is also made publicly available on our website. The contents of this Policy will be reviewed and updated as necessary and on at least an annual basis.

Procedure	• <u>Annual cycle</u>:
	   o Ou rData Privacy & Protection Lead supported by management will review and amend as appropriate the GDPR prep and maintenance project plan.
	
	• <u>Quarterly cycle:</u>
	   o Our Data Privacy & Protection Lead supported by management will review and amend as appropriate the GDPR prep and maintenance project plan.

Resources	<u>PRIMARY:</u> **ICO:** • https://ico.org.uk/for-organisations/guide-to-the-general-data-protection-regulation-gdpr/ • https://ico.org.uk/media/1624219/preparing-for-the-gdpr-12-steps.pdf **CIPD:** • https://www.cipd.co.uk/knowledge/fundamentals/people/hr/policies-factsheet <u>SECONDARY:</u> **External Consultant:** • https://www.linkedin.com/in/mauricebigmoflynn

Book:

- https://www.amazon.co.uk/-/e/B078ZGGLCW

Document Control Reference: GDPR - Issue No: v1.1 - Issue Date: xx/xx/2018 -Review Date: xx/xx/2019

Signature 1: *NAME 1* - Data Privacy & Protection Lead

Signature 2: *NAME 2* - Director

Company X Ltd., ADDRESS, UK +44 (0)TELEPHONE NUMBER.

Step 12: Guides & documentation

ICO Prep Steps	Risk Level	Resource Level	Action
1 Project Resource	High / Medium / Low	High / Medium / Low	Completed? Review cycle?
2 Data & Risk Audit	High / Medium / Low	High / Medium / Low	Completed? Review cycle?
3 Lawful Basis & Retention Records	High / Medium / Low	High / Medium / Low	Completed? Review cycle?
4 Consent & Legitimate Interest Compliance	High / Medium / Low	High / Medium / Low	Completed? Review cycle?
5 Privacy Policy	High / Medium / Low	High / Medium / Low	Completed? Review cycle?
6 Data Request Process	High / Medium / Low	High / Medium / Low	Completed? Review cycle?
7 Data Breach Process	High / Medium / Low	High / Medium / Low	Completed? Review cycle?
8 Data Transfers inc. International	High / Medium / Low	High / Medium / Low	Completed? Review cycle?
9 Kids & Special Category /Sensitive Data	High / Medium / Low	High / Medium / Low	Completed? Review cycle?
10 Privacy By Design	High / Medium / Low	High / Medium / Low	Completed? Review cycle?
11 Plan	High / Medium / Low	High / Medium / Low	Completed? Review cycle?
12 Awareness	High / Medium / Low	High / Medium / Low	Completed? Review cycle?

Document Control Reference: GDPR - Issue No: v1.1 - Issue Date: xx/xx/2018 -Review Date: xx/xx/2019

Signature 1: *NAME 1* - Data Privacy & Protection Lead

Signature 2: *NAME 2* - Director

Company X Ltd., ADDRESS, UK +44 (0)TELEPHONE NUMBER.

Hooray finished?

Not quite but it's a great start. GDPR and data privacy must be reviewed, revised and refreshed regularly to keep it front of mind and up to date for all.

Here's my tips for that ...

GDPR Adapt & Thrive! - Big Mo's Guide

Inspired by the ICO Guidelines

- Every **Moment** we **Think** "Personal Data is Private Data!"
- Every **Day** we **Watch** for data requests or breaches.
- Every **Week** we **Check** for GDPR news from the ICO.
- Every **Month** we **Diarise** a quick GDPR progress update.
- Every **Quarter** we **Delete** 2/5/7/? year old personal data.
- Every **Year** we **Audit** our "Privacy By Design" approach & update GDPR Documents plus check new partners for compliance.

https://thebigmoapproach.com

106

Be Better Business 2: Post GDPR

Whazzup?

Now that we're **up to speed with GDPR compliance**, let's take a look at our **digital channels and see how we can optimise** those further in a post GDPR world. **Some of this is relatively advanced,** based on the assumption that most companies have been using these channels for years. In all cases there are also **simpler improvements recommended - that all can benefit from - as well as intermediate and advanced improvement steps**.

What the experts say:

Based on our work with 1000's of companies, **most companies' digital channels can be significantly improved in 4 areas and those are: Reach, Cadence, Personalisation and Social Shares.** We'll explain these next in more detail and in the context of the main digital channels.

Too profitable?

There are several key ways to better engage customers and stakeholders: **Reach i.e % of target audience, Cadence i.e. timing, Personalisation of content and activating Social Sharing**. Most marketers **don't pull all**

these levers to the max and don't automate enough for **scalability**. Over the years email has been seen as a **niche tool** and it's also been **too profitable** for its own good. **Confusion over permission** hasn't helped. As a marketing practice it needs to **grow up and take its rightful leading place** at the business table. Email is a **key identifier** for the digital age - this has pro's and con's of course. Companies need to ensure their strategy is mature and **integrated.**

What the experts say:

See Big Mo's **eCRM Improvement Grid** below.

In this model we start with a **focus on conversions**. We develop profiles of conversions or near conversions i.e. **who/when/where/what/how led the conversions**? We then analyse the database to **find others on similar stages of the conversion journey** ie 90% complete vs 50% vs 20%. This allows us to **segment and prioritise our database** based on commercial targets and success probability. To align with GDPR rules we need to make sure we are completing the full **GDPR prep data minimisation**[78] **and risk management** stages.

---

[78] "What is Data Minimisation? | Experian." https://www.edq.com/uk/glossary/data-minimisation/. Accessed 11 Jun. 2018.

Post GDPR eCRM Improvement Grid:

a.FOR TARGET:	1. Better Reach	2.Better Cadence	3.Better Personalise
b.YOU NEED:	Better quality data partners	Time of send tool	Personalisation tool
c.EXAMPLE SOLUTIONS ARE:	Experian[79] Creditsafe[80] Acxiom[81] et al	Via email service provider ESP or manually	Via ESP partner (app) library
d.PLUS PREDICTIVE ANALYSIS:	Excel + Stats Extensions	Excel + Stats Extensions	Excel + Stats Extensions
e.I HAVE PROVEN THIS IN SECTORS:	Sport/Bet[82], All Retail[83], Travel[84], Finance, B2B, SME, Other	Sport/Bet, All Retail, Travel, Finance, B2B, SME, Other	Sport/Bet, All Retail, Travel, Finance, B2B, SME, Other

---

[79] "Experian." 22 Feb. 2017, https://www.experian.com/. Accessed 11 Jun. 2018.
[80] "Creditsafe: Business Credit Reports & Credit Score." https://www.creditsafe.com/us/en.html. Accessed 11 Jun. 2018.
[81] "Acxiom." https://www.acxiom.com/. Accessed 11 Jun. 2018.
[82] "The Jockey Club." http://www.jockeyclub.com/. Accessed 11 Jun. 2018.
[83] "Quidco." https://www.quidco.com/. Accessed 11 Jun. 2018.
[84] "Quidco." https://www.quidco.com/. Accessed 11 Jun. 2018.

Never enough?

It seems we never have enough content. **Yet we all create content all day long** when we speak to people, share opinions, write emails, post on Facebook and even show stuff with our hands and facial gestures. However when it comes to content creation for digital channels **all too often we panic** and think it's too hard, time consuming, costly or risky.

So what to do?

The approach we recommend here is to capture more of the day to day content that is created in every business and **use simple tools to spin that rough stuff into content gold**! This allows us to test the content to see which works best and therefore identifies **content strategies that have been proven to be worth focusing more time and resources on**.

What the experts say:

See Big Mo's **Content Improvement Grid** below.

In this model we start with a **focus on video**. One single video is a library of content in itself and can **feed clips, images, text articles, audio and more**. We do of course need **low cost simple tools** to slice and dice our video content. The tools I recommend below are mostly freemium i.e. we can **try them out for free and with no specialist skills needed.**

Big Mo's Post GDPR Content Improvement Grid:

a.FOR CONTENT:	Video	Text Images Audio Animation	Crisis
b.YOU NEED:	Always start with video	Audio tran scription & auto generation - edit & enhance	Replace content via dark site
c.EXAMPLE SOLUTIONS ARE:	Jing[85] GHangout[86] Live Youtube [87] FBInstagram [88]	MTurk[89] Wordsmith[90] EnhanceNet[91] Giphy [92] Animoto[93]	Wordpress[94] Pre crisis rehearse - Post crisis - SEO
d.PLUS PREDICTIVE ANALYSIS:	Excel + Stats Extensions	Excel + Stats Extensions	Excel + Stats Extensions
e.I HAVE PROVEN THIS IN SECTORS:	Marketing agencies	Marketing agencies	British Council

[85] "Jing | TechSmith." https://www.techsmith.com/jing-tool.html. Accessed 11 Jun. 2018.
[86] "Google Hangouts." https://hangouts.google.com/. Accessed 11 Jun. 2018.

[87] "Live Dashboard - YouTube." https://www.youtube.com/live_dashboard. Accessed 11 Jun. 2018.
[88] "Facebook Live." https://live.fb.com/. Accessed 11 Jun. 2018.

[89] "Amazon Mechanical Turk." https://www.mturk.com/. Accessed 11 Jun. 2018.

[90] "Wordsmith.org : The magic of words. word, language, quote, quotation ...." https://wordsmith.org/. Accessed 11 Jun. 2018.
[91] "AI method to upscale low-resolution images to high-resolution." 27 Oct. 2017, https://techxplore.com/news/2017-10-small-pixel-perfect-large.html. Accessed 11 Jun. 2018.
[92] "Giphy." https://giphy.com/. Accessed 11 Jun. 2018.

[93] "Animoto." https://animoto.com/. Accessed 11 Jun. 2018.
[94] "WordPress.com: Create a free website or blog." https://wordpress.com/. Accessed 11 Jun. 2018.

World domination?

Social media seems to have **taken over the world** at times - from elections to legal debates to celebrity culture and everything in between. The dominant platforms have **become mainstream** - the newer platforms will **often be bought up** before they can compete or alternatively drowned out. Of course the younger generation will always seek the **new, lower cost channels**.

OK what now?

Nowadays I look at social media as **simply more channels** for dialogue and engagement so the **questions to consider** become: are **your customers and stakeholders** there and if so what, if anything, **might they want from you there?** We need to download our data from social media platforms so we can **analyse it better and understand which content really works well i.e. drives commercial value and ROI**. Ads online allow you to boost your reach **once you know what the commercial value is**.

Expert Recommendation:

See Big Mo's **Social Improvement Grid** below.

The key here is to **extract our social media data** so we can incorporate it with data from other channels and build a **fully data picture of our conversions**. That way we know what to do next to get more conversions. If we don't extract the data while we can **it may become unavailable or more costly**. The data can be extracted

116

with a little code using the app **API gateway or else using a freemium tool** as mentioned.

Big Mo's Post GDPR Social Improvement Grid:

a.FOR IMPROVED::	Facebook Twitter	LinkedIn	Newer	Ads
b.YOU NEED TO:	Analyse what drives more positive engagement	Analyse what drives more positive engagement	Analyse what drives more to engage	Amplify success by using the algorithm
c.EXAMPLE SOLUTIONS ARE:	Extract data via FacebookApp [95] InstagramApp [96] TwitterApp[97]	Extract data via LinkedInApps[98]	Test and learn via Snapchat[99] Whatsapp [100] FBMessenger[101]	Facebook Google Amazon Ads[102]
d.PLUS PREDICTIVE ANALYSIS:	Excel + Stats Extensions	Excel + Stats Extensions	Excel + Stats Extensions	Excel + Stats Extensions
e.I HAVE PROVEN THIS IN SECTORS:	Sport/Bet, All Retail, Travel, Finance, B2B, SME, Other	Marketing Agencies	Marketing Agencies	Sport/Bet, All Retail, Travel, Finance, B2B, SME, Other

[95] "Facebook for Developers." https://developers.facebook.com/. Accessed 11 Jun. 2018.

[96] "Instagram API." https://www.instagram.com/developer/. Accessed 11 Jun. 2018.

[97] "Docs – Twitter Developers." https://developer.twitter.com/en/docs.html. Accessed 11 Jun. 2018.

[98] "LinkedIn Developer Network." https://developer.linkedin.com/. Accessed 11 Jun. 2018.

[99] "Snapchat - The fastest way to share a moment!." https://www.snapchat.com/. Accessed 11 Jun. 2018.

[100] "WhatsApp." https://www.whatsapp.com/. Accessed 11 Jun. 2018.

[101] "Messenger." https://www.messenger.com/. Accessed 11 Jun. 2018.

[102] "Amazon Advertising: Explore Amazon's advertising solutions." https://advertising.amazon.com/. Accessed 11 Jun. 2018.

Latest Insights

We'll focus again here on key drivers of customer and stakeholder growth and satisfaction: **reach, cadence and personalisation**. To do this best we need to **solve people's problems, engage them and answer their questions**, in a quick and compelling style. **Websites,**

blogs and apps therefore need to hyper personalise more. SEO is changing a lot with **audio, visual and even AI search,** so let's get the **basics right while we can**.

Expert Recommendation:

See Big Mo's **Web UX Improvement Grid** below.

Here we touch on several common opportunities across many companies:

- **SEO Search engine optimisation**[103]: This area is changing dramatically due to **new interfaces** (voice, visual etc.), **newer techniques** e.g. machine learning[104] and more. However in today's situation most companies I meet **still don't have a well constructed and extensive key word phrase target list**. Here below are some well established tools to help you do that.

- **Websites & blogs**: Should have been **personalised** a long time ago but a **creative rather than data led industry plus inertia** of the established players (web content management systems) have made it still a relative **rarity, beyond basic login systems with limited access to my personal history**. This is **changing as CMS and CRMs merge but the big software companies charge a lot** for what is technically well understood. My

---

[103] "Beginner's Guide to SEO (Search Engine Optimization) - Moz." 18 Dec. 2015, https://moz.com/beginners-guide-to-seo. Accessed 11 Jun. 2018.

[104] "Machine learning - Wikipedia." https://en.wikipedia.org/wiki/Machine_learning. Accessed 11 Jun. 2018.

recommendation is to **hack it together with some tech help** or if you have big budgets and limited time go to an SME provider.

- **Apps**: The majority of apps have **failed due to poor UX and/or the cost/complexity** of maintaining multiple different technologies (code bases). We can get better UX by using **codeless**[105] **app prototyping solutions** to get the UX right before we start to code. We can reduce costs and complexities with **web apps which are carefully optimised**[106] to mobile app infrastructures.

---

[105] "What's the top 10 list of code-less mobile app development ...." 8 Aug. 2015,
https://www.quora.com/Whats-the-top-10-list-of-code-less-mobile-app-development-platforms.
Accessed 11 Jun. 2018.
[106] "Progressive Web Apps | Web | Google Developers."
https://developers.google.com/web/progressive-web-apps/. Accessed 11 Jun. 2018.

Big Mo's Post GDPR Web UX Improvement Grid:

a.FOR TARGET:	1.Better Reach	2.Better Cadence/ Personalisation	3. Better Personalisation
b.YOU NEED:	SEO improvement via analytics & content	Web/blog improvement via personalisation	App with hyper personalisation
c.EXAMPLE SOLUTIONS ARE:	Keyword lists via GTrends[107] Adwords[108] Moz[109] Rich engaging content - see above.	Web CMS with login and iframes and/or content personalisation tools eg DECCO[110]	App UX prototype via Codeless[111] plus notifications gateway[112]
d.PLUS PREDICTIVE ANALYSIS:	Excel + Stats Extensions	Excel + Stats Extensions	Excel + Stats Extensions
e.I HAVE PROVEN THIS IN SECTORS:	Marketing Agencies	Sport/Bet, All Retail, Travel, Finance, B2B, SME, Other	Sport/Bet, All Retail, Travel, Finance, B2B, SME, Other

---

[107] "Google Trends." https://trends.google.com/trends/. Accessed 11 Jun. 2018.
[108] "Google AdWords." https://adwords.google.com/home/. Accessed 11 Jun. 2018.

[109] "Moz - SEO Software, Tools & Resources for ...." https://moz.com/. Accessed 11 Jun. 2018.

[110] "DECCO." http://www.decco-engine.com/. Accessed 11 Jun. 2018.

[111] "Codeless Platforms | Point and Click Software Solutions." https://www.codelessplatforms.com/. Accessed 11 Jun. 2018.
[112] "how to host my own push notification gateway ?? · Issue #8692 ...." 28 Oct. 2017, https://github.com/RocketChat/Rocket.Chat/issues/8692. Accessed 11 Jun. 2018.

2.5 The future and future proofing?

Trends "as big as the web"?

1. Machine learning via 'neural nets[113]';

2. Blockchain[114] for contracts and cryptocurrencies[115];

3. Man machine interfaces eg automotive sector.

Only one certainty ... continuous, ever faster change!

So my advice is to **lean on 'the machines'** where ever possible to keep up. The maths alone tells you there's **no other scalable way**.

I'm an optimist so here's to an even better future for all!

---

[113] "Artificial neural network - Wikipedia." https://en.wikipedia.org/wiki/Artificial_neural_network. Accessed 11 Jun. 2018.

[114] "Blockchain - Wikipedia." https://en.wikipedia.org/wiki/Blockchain. Accessed 11 Jun. 2018.
[115] "What is Cryptocurrency: Everything You Need To Know [Ultimate Guide]." https://blockgeeks.com/guides/what-is-cryptocurrency/. Accessed 11 Jun. 2018.

More about the author

Maurice 'Big Mo' Flynn - Fellow of the CIM IDM RSA and MEng Cantab

Maurice has **delivered learning events on these and related topics** for many of the biggest training companies in the UK, including the **CIM**[116]**, ISMM**[117]**, E-consultancy, DMA/IDM**[118]**, DMI**[119]**, IAB**[120] and more. At the **DMA/IDM** Maurice (with many others) has supported the expert council hubs, which help members optimise their marketing as well as prepare for GDPR. Over 30 years Maurice has trained tens of thousands of people at thousands of companies, including **Oracle, BBC, P&G and Google**. He also has worked as a **consultant on GDPR prep projects** for 50+ companies, large and small.

---

[116] "CIM | Qualifications, Training and ...." http://www.cim.co.uk/. Accessed 11 Jun. 2018.
[117] "Institute of Sales & Marketing Management | LinkedIn."
https://www.linkedin.com/showcase/institute-of-sales-&-marketing-management. Accessed 11 Jun. 2018.
[118] "Institute of Direct and Digital Marketing: Marketing Qualifications and ...." https://www.theidm.com/. Accessed 11 Jun. 2018.
[119] "Digital Marketing Institute: Digital Marketing Courses & Training."
https://digitalmarketinginstitute.com/en-us. Accessed 11 Jun. 2018.
[120] "IAB." https://www.iab.com/. Accessed 11 Jun. 2018.

He is married to his business partner Antoaneta and they have two young boys. Feel free to contact and follow 'Big Mo' via <u>LinkedIn</u> , <u>Eventbrite</u> and <u>Amazon</u> and most social media platforms.

Index

133